# PRAISE FOR TEENAGE WASTEBRAND

"You know an idea is great when it makes you think 'why didn't I think of that?' Evelyn hits it out of the park with a book that is thorough, relevant, and unique in the marketing world."
— Mark W. Schaefer, Best-selling author of
*KNOWN* and *Marketing Rebellion*

"Applying intuitive lessons from human adolescence to brand-building, Evelyn Starr's *Teenage Wastebrand* is a story-driven, example-rich, actionable read!"
— Whitney Johnson, Author of *Build an A Team*

"*Teenage Wastebrand* is a fun, easy-to-read, and practical guide to solving your brand's issues and cultivating brand leadership. Evelyn Starr's brand adolescence concept is an innovative lens for diagnosing why brands fail to scale and helping them get back on a growth track."
— Denise Lee Yohn, author of *What Great Brands Do* and
*FUSION: How Integrating Brand and Culture Powers
the World's Greatest Companies*

"Evelyn Starr shows you how to bust through walls and break through revenue plateaus. *Teenage Wastebrand* is a must read for entrepreneurs working to scale their businesses."
— Jeremy Miller, founder of Sticky Branding, author of
*Sticky Branding* and *Brand New Name*

"This is an entertaining, enjoyable, and useful book. It's extremely practical, chock full of examples, and anecdotes. It also contains numerous tips and suggestions. I highly recommend it to anyone interested in taking their brand to the next level."

—Dr. Graham Kenny, strategy expert and regular author in the *Harvard Business Review*

"Evelyn Starr illuminates how most brands enter an adolescence juncture, when a disparity emerges between original brand intent and brand evolution from your consumers' viewpoint. Decisions at this fork of the road after an initial run of success determine if brand growth continues, or conversely stalls or gets thrown into chaos and failure.

"From brands ranging from Netflix, Crocs, Lyft, and Facebook, to myriad entrepreneurs who all had to navigate these treacherous waters to move forward, Starr weaves engaging behind-the-scenes stories and pop culture references from hit teen movies with key brand growth principles. Starr offers a smart, highly actionable framework across all verticals of a business for getting unstuck - whether resolving a brand identity crisis, refining brand attributes, codifying your brand identity, moving beyond self-centeredness, or attracting the right consumers.

"A great must-read for everyone from seasoned CEOs to striving entrepreneurs!"

—Stacy DeBroff, CEO and founder, Influence Central

# TEENAGE
## WASTE *BRAND*

# How Your Brand Can STOP Struggling and START Scaling

Evelyn J. Starr

This publication is designed to provide accurate and authoritative information in regard to the subject matter covered. It is sold with the understanding that neither the author nor the publisher is engaged in rendering legal, accounting, or other professional service. If legal advice or other expert assistance is required, the services of a competent professional person should be sought.
*– From a Declaration of Principles jointly adopted by a Committee of the American Bar Association and a Committee of Publishers.*

E. Starr Associates
www.estarrassociates.com

First edition: March 2021

Publisher is not responsible for websites (or their content) that are not owned by the publisher.

Cover design and text layout by Clark Kenyon

Cover image from istockphoto.com

Author photo credit: Tracy Powell

Hardcover: ISBN 978-1736287200
Paperback: ISBN 978-1736287217
Large Print Paperback: ISBN 978-1736287224
Ebook: ISBN 978-1736287231
Audiobook: ISBN 978-1736287248

Library of Congress Control Number: 2020924817

*For Dan,*
*who always believed*
*I could write the Great American Novel*
*and is still waiting.*

# CONTENTS

# INTRODUCTION:

# It Was Going So Well until It Wasn't

I began my business as a corporate refugee in November 1999 when I was two months pregnant with my second child. My patience for endless meetings, face time, and office politics had run out.

I had not anticipated leaving my job, so I had no business plan. I contacted past colleagues and professional connections and offered freelance marketing research and strategy services, skills I had built during my years of working for consumer brands Veryfine Products, Dunkin' Brands, and The First Years. At the urging of a copywriter friend, I offered writing services too.

Gillette became my first client, signing on when I was eight months pregnant in April 2000. They were wonderful, helped my brand get started, and together we deepened a meaningful professional connection that still exists today.

For the next 10 years, connections and referrals helped me build a portfolio of marketing research, strategy, and copy-writing projects.

In 2008 my husband launched his own investment advisory firm. I got to help him build a brand from scratch. It was so exciting! We launched it on June 20, 2008.

Just in time for the financial crisis.

Happily, the brand withstood this early test and took root.

After things steadied for my husband's brand, I found myself in August 2009 needing to jumpstart my business pipeline and realizing that my 10-year-old brand was not as well-defined as the one I had just helped my husband create.

The cobbler's shoeless children, right? How could I be a self-respecting marketer without a well-defined brand? Being a generalist is the kiss of brand anonymity. I knew it was time to declare a niche, define my brand, and go deep.

But I struggled with what my niche would be. For 18 months I grappled with ideas. A marketing consultant colleague urged me to choose a food industry specialization based on my corporate experience, or focus on all new products or all existing products. Nothing felt right.

I felt uncomfortable in my own brand skin. It was as though the brand I thought I knew so well was actually a mystery to me.

On January 5, 2011 it came to me: my brand is having an identity crisis!

I could finally put a name to my feeling.

But wait — identity crisis?! That's crazy, I thought. That's usually the realm of teenagers.

## Teenage Memories Come Flooding Back

Nightmarish flashes of high school returned. Many classmates saw me as the nerdy girl who read every book assigned and took BC Calculus. The popular kids made fun of me. The class voted me "female class bookworm" in my senior year. My actions and values (reading and doing homework) defined my image in their eyes.

My friends — people who talked to me in class and spent time with me outside of class — had a different perspective. They admired my academic achievements and perseverance, appreciated my kindness and compassion, and smiled at my enthusiasm for the color purple and all things French. We came together as friends through shared values and mutual respect.

It dawned on me that my brain was replaying these visions because my brand needed to stand for something that would determine the clients I would attract, the same way my teenage image had attracted like-minded friends.

My brand needed an identity.

And, like high school, my audience's experience with me would shape that identity.

As I talked to other business owners, I discovered I was far from the only one feeling stuck. Growing pains abounded. Plateaus were common across the board, and often happened after the company's initial momentum stalled.

Researching resources, I could not find any that addressed this problem. Searching for brand development advice led to information on logo design and advertising messages. Brand gurus like David Aaker had much wisdom to share on brands conceptually, but none prescribed what to do when you are stuck in the space past your start-up years but before your business had established regular growth.

As I was falling asleep on Thursday January 20, 2011 at 11:45 pm, I had an epiphany.

What if brands had an adolescence like humans? What if instead of being fully formed from the start, they needed time to explore and find their identity? And what if they exhibited adolescent symptoms to signal this phase?

Like an identity crisis.

My curiosity piqued. After some test marketing of the concept proved it memorable and engaging, I began describing myself as specializing in work with "brands in adolescence," brands that had stalled after their initial success. I wanted to attract companies in this phase to see if my theory about brands having adolescent symptoms held true and to help them get unstuck.

This book is the result of what I've learned over nine years of studying brands, the way they develop, and why many of them get stuck after an initial burst of success.

In addition to working with clients who had brands in adolescence, I've conducted hundreds of hours of research and dozens of interviews. My research included reading thousands of articles and over a dozen books. I've reviewed hundreds of brand websites. Many business owners who approached me after hearing me speak shared their brand-in-adolescence frustrations and experiences as well.

To date I've analyzed over 160 brands ranging in size from sole proprietorships up to multibillion-dollar behemoths like Google and Facebook.

## What This Means for You and Your Brand

If your brand has stalled or plateaued after a good initial run, you are not alone. I've encountered many founders who launched businesses in the 1990s and 2000s who have hit a similar wall. Owners who knew their brands were capable of more and could envision that growth, but did not know how to scale the wall and get past it.

Brands experience growing pains akin to human adolescence and often exhibit similar symptoms. In this book I am going to show you what these symptoms look like. I'll help you diagnose your brand and then provide you with the path that can help you address the problem and get back to growth.

I am not trying to be cute or to play brand psychologist. Rather, I prefer straight talk to marketing jargon and have found the lens of adolescence helpful in understanding the hurdles brands face and how to address them.

As you read this book, you'll be able to see your brand's issues from a new perspective, one that is easy to relate to. If you've parented a teenager, you've already seen some of these symptoms in action. I'm not going to throw marketing speak at you, but rather describe each symptom and remedy in plain talk.

Symptoms of brands in adolescence include:

- Identity crisis
- Running with the wrong crowd
- Self-centeredness
- Suffering from FOMO and trying too hard to fit in
- A need to make new friends
- Defending a varsity team spot
- Oversleeping
- A need to assert independence

Not every stall or plateau signifies brand adolescence, however. Brands can encounter forces that might feel like brand adolescence but are not. These include:

- Economic downturns
- Technology shifts
- Entrepreneurial distraction

Brands can also experience growth spurts or find a sweet-spot size and decide to stay there.

In addition to showing you what your brand might be experiencing, you'll see examples of how others have faced similar predicaments. Brands you know like Airbnb, Zagat, and FedEx. Brands you may know like Spotify, Crocs, and Life is Good. Smaller brands you may not have heard of, but that have navigated — or are navigating — their adolescence and that will share how they surmounted those hurdles. I bet some of these brands share similarities with yours.

Knowing the problem gets you on the road to solving it. I'll take you further, with approaches to solving the problem based on the symptom your brand has. Like human adolescence, course correction is rarely done in a day, but brands are resilient and these actions can help you get your brand back to growth mode.

The sooner we start, the sooner you get your brand unstuck.

To begin, we need to talk about what a brand is from a human point of view to ensure we have a common perspective — and then we'll dive right into the symptoms.

Let's go!

# Part 1: Awkward Adolescence, It's Not Just For Humans Anymore

In order for us to have a productive discussion about your brand, we first need a common view of what a brand is.

As a business owner you might think of brands as images or entities that marketing creates. A logo you paid a designer for. A clever tagline. An ad campaign. But that's not what a brand is or how it is formed.

# CHAPTER 1

# A Brief Bit about Brands and Brand Adolescence

## How Brands Form

I spent the beginning of my career conducting market research and developing new products for three New England brands: Veryfine Juices, Dunkin' Donuts (now just Dunkin'), and The First Years. Anytime I mentioned where I worked, there was a good chance someone would volunteer an opinion or image of that company or of their products and services. I listened to these views with great interest.

Over time, I noticed people's views of the brand were the sum total of every experience they had ever had with it. Not just what they saw in the company's advertising or packaging, but every product usage or service encounter. And their memories were long.

The employee who always remembered their name and how they liked their coffee. The tang of their favorite flavor of juice. The ease of using a portable booster seat. All of those bode well for the brands.

Getting an order wrong. Spoiled or damaged products. Rude service. Those cast a pall on the brands.

Even if the company had no control over the outcome of the experience, people factored it in to their impression of the brand. For example, if the product was out of stock, people were disappointed not only in the retailer, but in the brand. If customers had a tough time parking at a restaurant, their ratings of their experience went down across the board, including quality of the food.

While detracting from the brand when it could not control the experience seemed unfair, I realized the more successful brands took this into account and tried to work with their partners to ensure a good experience. Fighting human nature was futile.

# We Brand to Survive

Humans' tendency to classify things is well documented.[1] Psychologists link this tendency to our earliest iteration as humans when we learned to assess an animal as predator or prey. Taking time to make that judgment could be the difference between finding dinner and being dinner.

Most brand encounters risk less dire outcomes now.

Few of us are dodging predators, but all of us are fielding an avalanche of communication. We don't have time to process every choice we face anew. Just to survive, we accumulate associations through experience with an entity — a brand — so the next time we encounter it, we have a reference point for action.

Oh yeah, that was the company that gave me free shipping on my return and a refund with no questions asked. I'll do business with them again. Or . . . that was the company that did not respond to my inquiry for a week. I'll not waste my time.

The more experiences you have with a brand, the more extensive and nuanced your image of it and your feelings toward it become.

# What is a brand?

*A brand is the expectation of what you will get when you interact with an entity based on prior experiences with, and impressions of, that entity.*

Note that the consumer or receiving party is doing the branding.

If you are doing business with people, you have a brand. Whether or not you've decided to have a brand, you've got one. Whether or not you've created a logo, penned a tagline, posted a website, or none of the above. You cannot stop people from gathering impressions associated with your brand name and storing them in a file in their brain.

# Brands Are Dynamic

If you are an entrepreneur and have launched your product, you had a shot upfront to tell the world what your brand sought to achieve. You named your brand, maybe set up some initial guidelines and staked out a competitive position. Or maybe you were like many founders, immersed in start-up mode, focused on gaining traction and generating cash flow to stay afloat. Maybe you didn't have the time to set guidelines or communicate your purpose beyond getting your offering off the ground.

Either way, you sent your brand baby into the world. Like a child though, once launched you cannot control your brand.

People have interactions with your brand unbeknownst to

you. They see your packaging, advertising, and social media posts; engage with your employees and distributors; shop for and use your products — all out of your view and earshot. The longer your brand is in the world, the more its audience has time to experience it and to formulate their image of it. Every interaction they have with it factors in.

As more and more people experience your brand and form an image, the image may migrate from your original intention. It is hard to know how your customers and your audience will perceive your brand and what aspects will dominate their impression.

In fact, it is likely that the majority of your brand's image does not come from your company at all.

A McKinsey study revealed that two-thirds of touchpoints during the active evaluation phase of a purchase come from consumer-driven marketing activities like reviews; word-of-mouth recommendations from friends, family, and social media connections; in-store interactions; and recollections of past experiences.[2]

Even the one-third of touchpoints that does come from company-driven marketing gets filtered through the customer's lens: whether they found it believable, whether they liked it, or whether it offended them. It's hard to know exactly how your messages are perceived, internalized, and stored.

## What Causes Brand Adolescence?

If you have guided your brand past start-up mode and have been in the marketplace long enough to see significant growth, then your brand has had plenty of time for the world to weigh in with their impressions and influence it.

A brand is thrust into adolescence by the disparity between what the original brand was intended to be or how it entered the world and what it has developed into. Some of the reasons this migration occurs can include:

- The brand team is no longer just you with the idea, but several people who have brought their own ideas and values to the brand.

- Experience with your offerings has created a particular image in the minds of your audience, which may emphasize different attributes and aspects of the brand than what you thought would be the most salient ones.

- Your offerings have migrated or expanded from your original products to reflect customer requests and needs. Your product portfolio differs from what it was in the beginning.

- Reviews of your products have recommended your brand for strengths different from the ones you have emphasized.

- Word of mouth has spread and taken your brand to markets you did not foresee or in an order you did not forecast.

- Operational scaling has hit the brand with challenges that require new approaches, new systems, and new hires.

Growth challenges brands. Early on, brands can accommodate growth just by adding a little more talent here, a few more raw materials there. Successful brands hit a juncture, though, when the gap from where the brand started and where it needs to be to continue growing has widened beyond incremental adjustments.

The gap can be in marketing messages — the original that no longer resonates and the unknown message that will drive sales now.

The gap can be in operations — the original production setup has maxed out and the brand needs a bigger space, more employees, a new system, or maybe all of the above to continue to meet demand.

The gap can be in customer experience — between what the customer expected when they placed the order and what they got in delivery. Or in solving any issues with delivery.

The gap can be in employee experience — between what the brand claimed about its culture and work environment during the recruitment process and what the employee actually experiences.

In his book *Marketing Rebellion: The Most Human Company Wins*, Mark W. Schaefer reports that,

"Businesses believe 81 percent of their marketing messages are relevant and useful, in contrast with 84 percent of consumers who say these communications are NOT useful at all!"

"Businesses say they're slow to respond to consumers about 25 percent of the time, but consumers disagree and contend that businesses are slow 83 percent of the time."

"Businesses think just 13 percent of their marketing messages are unsolicited, while consumers feel 85 percent of the messages they receive from businesses are spam."[3]

If your perception of your brand differs from that of your customers, you are clearly not alone!

Potential gaps exist in all areas of the brand and when the existing fabric of the brand has stretched to a breaking point in one or more gaps, growth can slow, stall, plateau, or even decline.

Brand adolescence is the first time this occurs, as these problems are often caused by missing elements or actions that are necessary for the brand to mature.

Like human adolescence, brand adolescence is a growth stage that can exhibit a range of symptoms. Brands can:

- **Have an identity crisis** by lacking a clear purpose and defined attributes that resonate with customers and are understood and implemented by everyone on the brand team.

- **Run with the wrong crowd** by targeting an audience that is either too small to support the brand or one that does not value what the brand offers.

- **Be self-centered** by putting management's interests before customer needs and concerns.

- **Try too hard to fit in** by chasing what other brands are doing instead of finding a niche it can own and standing for something specific.

- **Need to make new friends** by maxing out its initial target audience or losing them for some reason.

- **Need to defend their position** by proving a niche that is viable and lucrative enough to attract a lot of competitors.

- **Oversleep** by ignoring industry developments and market trends.

- **Assert their independence** by growing to the point where their leader no longer has the skill set or interest in the management needed to lead them through the next level of growth.

If at least one of these brand adolescent symptoms resonates with you, feel free to dive right into Part 2 which explains each symptom in detail.

If none of these resonate or if you are unsure, it is possible that your brand is being a typical obstinate teenager and refusing to be categorized. Or that your brand is not in adolescence, but stalling or plateauing for another reason.

# CHAPTER 2

# Scenarios That May Masquerade as Brand Adolescence, but Are Not

W hile brand adolescence symptoms are common for brands that stall after their initial run, they are far from the only reason your brand might be stuck. Other forces and factors might look like brand adolescence because they coincide with your brand's first plateau. In this chapter, I'm going to touch on five other reasons your brand might be stuck at this juncture. If one of these rings a bell for you, brand adolescence is not your problem.

## Economic Downturns

Economic downturns can thrust brands that are thriving into chaos. Take, for example, Bob Van Andel, who had to get creative to save his fledging software product business.

In the mid-1990s as the internet was surging, device management required either a human present to enact commands or a master console that would send messages to the device and receive the responses. In 1995, Bob got the idea to create an embedded web server that allowed the user to interact with the device — a printer, for example — using a graphic interface over a web browser.

Bob incorporated Allegro Software Development Corporation in February 1996 and launched the product with a partner.

Xerox became a customer early on, putting Allegro's embedded server into their printers and other products. Allegro charged a separate license for each product.

Business was robust early on. Bob opened a bottle of Champagne to celebrate each sale. In year three, he shifted to once-a-quarter celebrations as new sales had grown too much to celebrate individually.

Allegro was five years old when the dot-com bubble burst in March 2001, throwing the US economy into recession. Since the company sold device management to internet hardware companies, there was a lag until those companies felt the effect of the burst bubble. Allegro's sales level held on until the second quarter of 2002.

The recession highlighted a key problem with Allegro's model: selling product-specific licenses meant the company only made money when customers launched products. It was hard to predict when the next product license would come along.

The company tightened its belt, but revenue kept shrinking. Some customers who had licensed Allegro's device management products defaulted before their planned company saw the light of day. By 2004 things looked grim.

Bob's plan for Allegro to survive was to propose a shared pain to keep the team together rather than let someone go. Everyone took a pay cut in May 2004. Bob kept track of employees' pay sacrifices.

Meanwhile, in 2003, Allegro introduced a product line for consumer electronic products. Instead of licensing them, Allegro offered them via subscription, creating a regular revenue stream.

In 2005 Allegro's customer electronic product line began to take off and the company turned around. By the end of December 2005, Bob repaid Allegro's employees. His plan saved the company.

By 2008 they had contracted enough subscriptions to generate sufficient income to make enduring the Great Recession easier than the one in 2001.

Economically trying times demand cool-headed actions to keep your brand viable. These conditions are out of your control and not a brand-in-adolescence symptom.

# The Technology Brand Treadmill

The speed of innovation causes technology brands to mature faster and in a different manner from other industries. Tech brand teams can feel like they are running at full speed and still fighting to get unstuck from a brand growth plateau. The threat of obsolescence means tech brands can quickly become irrelevant. Shifts to new technological platforms to stay relevant can slow growth.

This is not to say that technology brands don't have an adolescence. They often do, and at a younger age than other industries. The fast pace of technology accelerates brand maturation, making tech brand years more like dog years than human ones.

Keeping up with the technology industry is hard and expensive, however plateaus due solely to technological changes are not a brand-in-adolescence problem, but a fact of life for those in the tech industry.

Netflix is a prime example.

In 1997, Reed Hastings and Marc Randolph founded Netflix to free consumers from defined television schedules by providing on-demand entertainment. Initially the delivery of on-demand entertainment was physical, mailing requested DVDs to subscribers which eliminated their need to leave the house. DVDs were a new technology at the time.

Though Netflix led with DVD mailings, Hastings claims to have known from early on that delivery would eventually be over the internet. DVD sales and rentals peaked in 2006.[4] Netflix launched their streaming service in 2007 when the brand was 10 years old.

Migrating to delivery via a streaming service was necessary for Netflix to remain competitive, as consumers were shifting toward online viewing and away from DVDs.

If you have a tech brand that has stalled because your market is migrating to a new technological foundation, that is a tech industry issue and not brand adolescence.

## Entrepreneur/Owner Evolution

Successful entrepreneurs are often serial entrepreneurs, with diverse interests and a proclivity for the start-up phase of a project or brand. If you feel your brand is stuck, this could be a function of your interests migrating — or wanting to migrate — to your next project.

Mary Adams knows this sensation well.

In 1998, Mary launched Trek Consulting to guide business owners on strategy and growth by helping them with financing. Her husband joined the venture.

Five years later, they learned of the concept of intangible capital (IC) and the need to incorporate tough-to-measure brand assets into the company's valuation. Experts in Sweden trained them in the concept, and they developed methodologies to sell IC as a service.

The business Mary was conducting differed enough for her to found a separate brand called Intangible Capital [IC]. Trek Consulting's work slowed and went into a holding pattern.

"Trek's problem was that I got interested in IC [Intangible Capital] — it sapped the energy for the other things,"[5] Mary told me.

Ultimately, in 2013, Mary folded Trek Consulting and Intangible Capital into a single new brand called Smarter Companies.

But Mary's interests still exceeded the Smarter Companies brand umbrella. She founded two other organizations — the Exit Planning Exchange in 2012 and the Integrated Reporting US Community in 2017 — and currently divides her time between the three brands.

Serial entrepreneurs like Mary often create strong brands, but lose interest as they discover the next fertile area of unmet needs — "white space" that they are magnetically drawn to. Savvy serial entrepreneurs prevent their brands from suffering by either putting resources in place to keep them growing and healthy or by stepping aside.

If your brand has stalled and you find your interest lies elsewhere, it might be time for you to either recommit to your brand or to get someone else to lead it. This is not a brand-in-adolescence issue, it's a leadership one.

## Growth Spurts

All your brand metrics might grow in tandem in the early days. Number of customers, total sales, average order size, number of distribution points, and other measures rise fast in start-up mode. Once you have established your brand well enough that cash flow worries aren't keeping you up at night however, your brand growth may become less uniform.

If your brand has stalled in sales, are there other areas where it has grown? Maybe it isn't stalled overall. Maybe your brand is just experiencing growth spurts in some areas in preparation for later growth in others, like a child who gains weight and girth before inching taller. You might need to look beyond sales to see the growth.

Analyze your other metrics.

Did you serve more customers than the prior period? Perhaps new customers made a small purchase to try your brand, leveling your sales but expanding your audience size.

Have you increased your distribution points, perhaps diverting your attention from current sales to prepare for more sales later?

Did you hire and train more staff to gain capacity for more sales and service in the future?

All three of these situations qualify as growth, and they are not the only ways a brand can expand while revenue remains level. For most brands, smart growth means concentrating in some areas, but not all at once, to build a solid foundation. Trying to scale fast in all areas can scatter brand efforts and deliver a less-than-desired brand experience.

Growth spurts are a normal part of brand expansion, not an adolescent brand bane.

# Lifestyle Business

Capitalist societies prize size and speed. Many believe if your brand isn't growing, it's dying. But that's not always true. Some business owners have chosen to "right-size" their businesses to meet their goals and to live their lives on their own terms.

Stacy DeBroff, owner of Influence Central, built her brand that way.

From 1998 to 2005, Stacy published four books, "to help Moms solve issues that bogged them down."[6] She also launched the website MomCentral.com. The books and website established Stacy as a Mom market expert. Public relations firms sought Stacy as a spokesperson for the Mom-focused brands they represented.

Stacy foresaw that nascent social media would give influencers a mechanism to sway consumers just as she had. "I saw the market opportunity, that influencers were going to rise and to dominate conversations."[7]

Stacy launched Mom Central Consulting in 2007 and bootstrapped the business.

In their first year, Mom Central reached $1 million in revenue, and grew by $1 million each of the next seven years. Her success in reaching moms had prompted clients to ask for access to influencers for other desirable markets. In 2014 Stacy launched the umbrella brand Influence Central which comprised Mom Central Consulting, Dad Central Consulting, Millennial Central, and Influence Central Canada.

Mom Central and then Influence Central made the Inc. 5000 list five times between 2011 and 2015.

In 2015 Influence Central reached $8 million in revenue. In 2016 the brand hit a plateau. To grow beyond the $8 million mark Stacy realized she would need to take outside funding, and she had no interest in that. "People can be derogatory about lifestyle business, but if I wanted to be bigger I would need to take capital. They [investors] would dilute and intrude on my vision."[8]

Stacy keeps Influence Central self-funding by maintaining a lean team and taking only projects that are a good fit for the firm.

Lifestyle business owners have clarity on the business's purpose, on their values, and on how they want to spend their time. They find their sweet-spot size — where they can serve customers, support employees, fulfill their purpose, and live their values — and stay there to keep their good thing going.

If your brand has plateaued, but is viable, stable, and affording you the lifestyle you want, perhaps you have a lifestyle business. If you like where your brand is and can sustain it, you don't have to grow it further.

Lifestyle businesses are a choice and a solid brand construct. Lifestyle businesses that have found their sweet spot are not stuck like brands in adolescence, but are often thriving and making their owners happy in the process.

If your brand situation falls into one of the above categories — Economic Downturn, Tech Brand Treadmill, Owner Distraction, Growth Spurts, or Lifestyle Business — you do not have a brand in adolescence.

If you have yet to find the reason your brand is stuck, come with me to Part 2 where we explore brand-in-adolescence symptoms and see if any of those resonate for you.

# Part 2: Brand Adolescence Symptoms & Remedies

As we dive into the eight symptoms of brand adolescence I have discovered, please feel free to jump to the symptom that is afflicting your brand. Each chapter begins with a "Signs Your Brand Is . . . " section. If two or more of the signs ring true for your brand, that symptom might be the culprit behind your brand's stall — or at least a contributor.

Few brands mature without experiencing at least one of these symptoms. They don't discriminate by industry or geography. They plague business-to-consumer (B2C), business-to-business (B2B), and direct-to-consumer (D2C) brands alike, both product-focused and service-driven brands.

It is possible for a brand to suffer from more than one symptom at once. If that's your brand, and Identity Crisis is one of your symptoms, address that first. Then pick off the remaining symptoms with a long-term view of what will help you most next. If you are unsure, follow the order of the chapters.

It's also possible for you to remedy one brand adolescence symptom and have another emerge in the future, or to discover more symptoms once you've addressed the first.

I've put the Identity Crisis symptom first as this is most common. After that, the symptoms are sequenced by the remedy's contribution to your brand's foundation.

Each chapter includes help on how to address the symptom. The remedies in total comprise a set of tools that most long-term successful brands have created and use daily. Even if your brand is not suffering, it may benefit from them if you don't have these tools in place. You might even be able to dodge symptoms by creating them proactively!

# CHAPTER 3

# Having an Identity Crisis

## Signs Your Brand Has an Identity Crisis

If you find yourself nodding "Yes" to two or more of these signs, your brand may be having an identity crisis.

- Do you wonder why your customers choose your brand over your competitors?

- Do you have a hard time explaining to prospects what differentiates your brand from your competitors?

- Do you struggle with marketing messages or feel like you are always starting with a blank slate?

- Do your ads and marketing efforts lack an obvious theme or consistent message?

- Do you agonize over new product offering decisions and feel it is unclear which direction you should go?

> • Do you second-guess or revisit your product and marketing message decisions even after they have been made?

## Who Do You Think You Are?

Five teenagers arrive at their high school at 7 am. A glamour girl with perfect makeup. A clean-cut nerd. A muscular guy donning a varsity team jacket. A ruffian in sunglasses. A goth girl whose unkempt hair partially covers her suspicious black-rimmed eyes.

But it's Saturday. The halls are empty. They make their way to the library, but they are not there to study. And they are not happy to be there. They are in detention.

As penance for their various transgressions, the Assistant Principal has compelled them to a nine-hour confinement during which they are to reflect on their wrongdoing and write a 1,000-word essay on "who you think you are."

You might recognize this as the opening to the 1985 movie *The Breakfast Club*.

As the characters begin to interact, it is clear each of them sees the others as the stereotypes they embody. Yet their conversation over the day reveals that none of them wants to be thought of as a stereotype, and all of them share universal struggles like contentious relationships with their parents.

In the end, the "brain" character, Brian, delivers a single 97-word letter to the Assistant Principal on behalf of the group:

*Dear Mr. Vernon,*

*We accept the fact that we had to sacrifice a whole Saturday in detention for whatever it is that we did wrong. But we think you're crazy to make us write an essay telling you who we think we are.*

*You see us as you want to see us, in the simplest terms, in the most convenient definition.*

*But what we found out is that each one of us is a brain and an athlete and a basket case, a princess and a criminal.*

*Does that answer your question?*

*Sincerely yours,*

*The Breakfast Club*[9]

The movie struck a chord with adolescents everywhere, including me. I was 19 when it came out. I related to the characters and their struggles. I loved the movie despite the crucial error that ruined my favorite character.

*The Breakfast Club* continues to gain an audience with teens. Anna Kendrick's character in the 2012 movie *Pitch Perfect* is so moved by the movie's ending that she cries.

Why does *The Breakfast Club* resonate so strongly with teens? Because almost every teen wrestles with their identity.

## What Is an Identity Crisis?

German-American developmental psychologist Erik Erikson coined the term "identity crisis," defining it as the struggle in adolescence to find a balance between developing a unique, individual identity while still "fitting in" with peers. Solving the crisis requires that the adolescent decide who they want to be and how they want to be perceived.

Few teens pass through adolescence without an identity crisis. Struggles with the crisis can involve much trial and error, and can be painful to observe.

This is true for brands too. Defining a brand's identity can be tough, especially when the first attempts don't pan out. But done right, it can lead to clearer direction, easier priority setting and decision-making, and steadier, more reliable growth.

## Crocs' Meteoric Ride and Slide

Lyndon "Duke" Hanson, Scott Seamans, and George Boedecker founded Crocs™ in 2002. The three sold the clogs at a boat show in the beginning, due to their resin-made, water-resistant utility. But the shoes appealed to restaurant and hospital workers too, and soon took off.[10]

The resin they used, branded Croslite, was lightweight, resisted odor and fungus, and used body heat to conform to the wearer's footprint. These properties made Crocs incredibly comfortable, hence their appeal to anyone who spent hours on their feet each day.

By 2006 Crocs had soaring success, raising over $200 million from the largest US shoe company initial public stock offering and reporting $354.7 million in revenue, triple the revenue of 2005.[11]

Crocs were ugly, but they were everywhere. For fans, comfort trumped fashion. From Nordstrom, mall kiosks, and Crocs-branded stores to pharmacies and gift shops, you could nab a pair anywhere. In 2007, Crocs hit $850 million in sales and netted $200 million in profit.

Fashion industry commentators acknowledged that they had become a full-blown fad.

A year later, the brand lost $200 million. Having oversaturated their market, they were no longer special. Management blamed the recession, but at only $30 a pair, that was unlikely to be the primary reason for their troubles.

To boost the brand, management launched several new styles and announced global expansion plans. The all-out effort lifted profit to $150 million in 2011, but they soon found the brand flailing again. On July 14, 2014, they announced 183 layoffs and closed 100 of their 600 stores.

Like the new kid in high school who edits clothing and behavior to conform to each clique they encounter, Crocs tried to appeal to everyone and had no clear appeal to anyone. Without an obvious stance and personality, Crocs' audience was free to perceive the brand any way they wanted to.

Few remained neutral in their opinion. People either loved or hated them.

Crocs' fans loved their practicality and raved about their comfort.

But haters were more vocal, accusing the brand of being ugly and unfashionable. Some raged in diatribes on blogs or by making videos of themselves burning Crocs or cutting them up. The brand became the butt of jokes and the victim of bullying.

At 13 years old, Crocs was a typical brand in adolescence having an identity crisis.

# Dangers of Identity Crisis: Random Performance, Anguished Decision-Making, Wasted Resources

Brands that lack identity leave themselves open to criticism and unwanted associations. Their teams end up reacting to counter these notions. They spend valuable time fighting these fires at the expense of growing the brand.

Lack of identity also makes it hard for the brand team to make crucial decisions like which products to offer, what marketing messages to use, how to reach their audience, and what growth opportunities or partnerships to pursue. There are no guidelines to help them decide. Management can be left feeling like it is guessing what the right thing to do is, or gambling on a direction instead of knowing which one makes sense. Return on investment suffers as guessing leads to failed products, ineffective marketing, and other poor decisions.

Undefined brands have trouble unifying their teams, as each employee has their own idea of what the brand is. Without a common identity, teams often lack cohesiveness and the motivation to work together. Employees sometimes substitute their own agenda when the brand's purpose is unknown, which results in friction, random and counterproductive investments, and wasted time.

Because there are no guidelines, customers' experiences with the brand vary. Marketing fails to communicate a consistent and meaningful message. Product and service quality are unpredictable. Customer service helpfulness depends on who the customer talks to and their personal level of dedication to the brand. It is hard for customers to know what to think about the brand or why it might be the right choice for them. This uncertainty reduces the chances they will opt for it in the future.

Random decision-making, uncertain employees who don't know how best to work and what they are working toward, and customers' muddied images of the brand create an internal turbulence. In turn, this makes for stalled growth and declining revenues.

After riding the erratic brand growth rollercoaster for the first 12 years, Crocs knew they had to gain some measure of control over their brand identity to survive in the long term.

## Crocs' Identity Crisis Solution Attempt #1

When I wrote about Crocs in February 2015, I recommended that they should anchor their identity to their comfort characteristic, and that they should seek to market the emotional benefits of the brand. For example, the joy of wearing something that supports and does not hurt your feet, or the peace of mind knowing the shoes will always be in good working condition due to their indestructible nature. Consumer research would provide insight here.

I did not know that while they were cutting losses and closing stores in 2014, Crocs had also embarked on the path to self-discovery. Unfortunately, like many adolescents' first attempts, it was the wrong path.

Launched in March 2015 with ad agency McKinney Global, Crocs' "Find Your Fun" campaign centered on amusement. It featured breezy images of swimming pools and other environments shaped like the brand's iconic clog, along with videos of people dancing and playing in their Crocs shoes.

Watching other people have fun was just that. Watching.

The campaign did not engage the hearts of its customers. Nor did it help the brand define its identity sufficiently to emerge from its crisis. After an initial bump in revenue, year-over-year sales declined 6.3 percent in the second quarter of 2016 and 11.6 percent in the third. By the second half of 2016, the "Find Your Fun" campaign had fizzled.

Crocs management went back to the drawing board, hired a new agency (Yard), and developed a new campaign.

## Crocs Finds Their Footing

This time, Crocs embraced comfort, not only physically but psychologically. They played on the idea of being comfortable in one's own shoes.

Crocs' "Come As You Are" campaign launched in April 2017 and proclaimed the brand's pride in being just who they are. The campaign tapped celebrities who could relate to being unique and who appealed to Crocs' target market countries — the United States, Japan, China, Korea, and Germany.

Actor Drew Barrymore talked about how the message of inclusion was important to her as the mother of two young children. Singer and actor Yoona was drawn to the campaign's spirit of "overcoming preconceived notions." Entertainer Henry Lau said he felt the campaign was "about celebrating everything you've gone through — the good and the bad."

WrestleMania star Jon Cena talked openly about being bullied when he was 14 years old and how it led to him finding his passion.

The "Come As You Are" campaign resonated with customers, some of whom posted pictures of themselves on social media wearing their clogs all over the world.

At the same time, Crocs' management developed a plan to

become leaner operationally, closing 160 underperforming company stores between 2017 and 2018, bringing their total to fewer than 400. The company also outsourced production and reduced its global product line to focus on the most profitable offerings.

In contrast to their emergency-mode 2014 store closures and layoffs, these company store reductions and the departure from company-owned production facilities reflected careful thought about the brand's strengths. Brand leaders assessed it as less about operating retail stores and manufacturing, and more about innovation and design. In an August 10, 2018 message to media outlet Mashable, a company representative stated, "Crocs will continue to innovate, design, and produce the most comfortable shoes on the planet."[12]

Playing to their strengths, Crocs posted revenue increases in 2017 and 2018 despite significantly fewer stores and the charges that came with closing them. They also shifted emphasis to their ecommerce and wholesale channels.

## Brand Identity = Purpose + Attributes

Erikson said adolescents get through their identity crisis by deciding who they want to be and how they want to be perceived. Brands solve their identity crises the same way.

"Who you want to be" is your brand's purpose in the world. Your brand's attributes signal "how you want to be perceived."

To solve your brand's identity crisis, you need to define its purpose and determine its attributes.

# Your Purpose Is What Your Brand Wants to Be

A brand purpose is a short statement that describes what your brand wants to be. Your brand's reason for being addresses the problem it solves for your customers and, these days, for the world. It is often the reason the business was started in the first place.

Successful brands have clarity on their purpose. Some you might recognize include:

**Life is Good:** To spread the power of optimism.

**Nike:** To bring innovation and inspiration to every athlete in the world.

**Google:** To organize the world's information and make it universally accessible and useful.

**Airbnb:** To create a world where Anyone can Belong Anywhere.

**Kickstarter:** To help bring creative projects to life.

**The North Face:** To provide the best gear for our athletes and the modern day explorer, support the preservation of the outdoors, and inspire a global movement of exploration.

**L.L. Bean:** To sell goods and services that allow people to get outside and enjoy the outdoors.

In Crocs' case, their self-discovery process led them to adopt their brand message as their stated purpose: "Crocs is dedicated to the future of comfort."

While it might take time to find your brand's purpose, once discovered it will rarely change. Brand purposes don't shift with the wind, but stake a claim on territory that your brand wants to own for the long haul.

A well-crafted brand purpose:

- **Solves a real problem.** Crocs' buyers need shoes they can wear for hours without hurting their feet. Nike buyers want to improve their athletic performance. Google users need to find answers to very specific queries without having to comb through thousands of information sources.

- **Transcends an individual product.** While many companies are founded on the basis of a single product or service, to make the leap to an established brand your purpose has to be bigger than that. Crocs was founded with the launch of their signature clogs, but the clogs are not the whole of the brand. Comfort is — in different iterations.

    Airbnb started as overflow lodging for conferences. The brand now offers a sense of belonging anywhere via accommodations, experiences, and host communities. L.L. Bean began with a boot and now provides hundreds of products centered on encouraging outdoor enjoyment.

    Product-based purposes risk irrelevance in the face of competition, technological changes, new trends, and regulatory risks.

- **Is timeless.** Brand purposes should center on a solution to a recurring or ongoing human problem, need or desire. People will be pursuing comfort, athletic performance, information, and a sense of belonging as long as we exist on this earth, giving

Crocs, Nike, Google, and Airbnb much running room
to serve those needs and desires.

- **Resonates emotionally.** Beloved brands become
  beloved by striving to do something that is meaningful
  to their audience — employees, customers, owners,
  distributors, vendors, everyone who engages with
  the brand in some way. The desire to be accepted
  — and celebrated — for who we are is a widespread
  emotion. Crocs buyers might also seek a way to express
  themselves, and wearing something that signifies
  being comfortable in their own shoes is part of that
  self-expression.

  Kickstarter donors might see themselves as patrons
  of innovation and art. The North Face customers
  might self-associate with explorers, those who conquer
  ambitious goals, and those who support nature
  preservation.

- **Needs little follow-up explanation.** Most importantly,
  brand purposes communicate what the brand is about
  to all its constituencies. Purposes need to be clear,
  concise, easy to understand, easy to remember, and
  easy to execute. That's why Life is Good, Airbnb, and
  Kickstarter have purposes fewer than 10 words, yet we
  know exactly what they do.

## Brand Purpose Anchors Your Company

Your brand purpose is not a flowery statement that you proclaim
to the world. It is a powerful guiding force for your brand, helping

you communicate what your brand is about and make decisions about everything your business does. It has implications for every aspect of the business: the products the brand offers, the messages it conveys, the way the company operates.

A clear brand purpose becomes a source of inspiration as it makes it easy for employees at all levels of the organization to understand what they are working toward and to focus on activities that serve that purpose. Your brand purpose provides a litmus test for all considered company activities and makes it easy to determine which opportunities are "on brand" and which the company should pass on.

In Crocs' eight-word statement, "Crocs is dedicated to the future of comfort," we know that toe-pinching stilettos are not going to be in their line-up. That's an easy decision for them. In their dedication to comfort, Crocs is also sending a message to current and future employees that their culture is inclusive and encourages people to be themselves.

That is not to say that having a well-designed brand purpose prevents the company from making mistakes, but it vastly decreases this risk and can facilitate course correction when errors happen.

In Google's quest, "To organize the world's information and make it universally accessible and useful," they have launched hundreds of products and services. Over time, their portfolio ballooned and stretched their resources too far. To get back on track and survive their brand adolescence, they pared their portfolio by 224 offerings as of February 2021,[13] including Google+, Picasa, Google Reader, Inbox by Gmail, and Google Cloud Connect. Google stays on track and innovative by not being afraid to try new services and nixing the ones that don't pan out or that prove less useful to their purpose.

The power of a purpose can propel a brand forward if it remains true to its vision. Brands that proclaim a purpose for show but operate in a manner inconsistent with their purpose lose credibility, which is hard to win back.

Facebook might proclaim that they care about users' data privacy and preventing fake news. But the brand's minimum action since the discovery of major data breaches and lack of action against obviously fake news, like the doctored video of Nancy Pelosi in May 2019, have not fooled users. Per the 2020 Axios Harris Poll of the US's Most Visible 100 Companies, Facebook's reputation fell from #51 in 2018 to #97 in 2020.

# Finding Your Brand's Purpose

The first step to solving your brand's identity crisis is to find your brand's purpose. (The second is to determine its attributes, which we will get to later in this chapter.)

Your brand's purpose is its "why." Done well, it serves as your organization's guiding force. You might have heard terms like "vision" and "mission," but I like to keep things simple: your brand's purpose is the singular guiding force you need.

Given the central and strategic role your brand's purpose plays, it makes sense to dedicate the time you need to get it right. Depending on the size of your organization, finding your purpose can take from a couple of weeks to a couple of months. This investment will pay off indefinitely.

Your path to finding your purpose takes you away from the brand at first. Here are the steps:

1. **Take a break from the business and get away from the office.** Every business owner I spoke to agreed that the

day-to-day needs of the business and the worn groove of regular routines made it hard to see your business's big picture. Find a way to step back for a while — a true break, like a vacation. Clear your head.

Naomi Dunford, the owner of Ittybiz.com, went through a traumatic brand identity crisis (more about that below), and advised, "Go away for a two-week retreat in the Bahamas, shutter the place, go away and get refreshed. Whatever it costs, it's worth it. Brands in adolescence, we are afraid that we can't stop driving, we can't step away, we can't sustain certain losses. We get weighed down by our 'we can'ts.' Most are survivable. Do absolutely whatever it takes to get away, get some perspective, and come back fresh."[14]

Even if you can't afford two weeks in the Bahamas, take a real break from the business before you proceed.

2. **Revisit the reason you started or took over the business.** After you have had time to clear your head, but while you are still away from the business, recall your original inspiration and intention.

Mary Adams, founder of Smarter-Companies and consultant specializing in Intangible Capital, recommends, "going back to who you are and what's the problem the company solves? Getting true toward that."[15]

I recommend writing down your answers to the following questions:

Why did you get into the business in the first place?
What problem were you trying to solve?
What did you set out to achieve in the industry?
What were your goals?

Writing out your responses helps you clarify your thoughts. Answer these questions as well as you can and don't rush to be done. Mulling things over for a few days or even a week might lead to additional and deeper insights.

3. **Do an off-site meeting with your key employees.** After you have cleared your head and reminded yourself why you started the brand, you might want to involve key and longtime employees who you feel serve the brand well in this exercise.

   It is crucial to involve key employees if your brand is more than you and just supporting staff, more than 5-10 people, and especially if your brand involves other customer-facing employees. If your brand started as a hobby or has migrated from its early iteration, they might be able to provide insights you may not have yourself.

   It can be tempting to bypass involving your team to save time. You might be eager after your retreat to just act on your revelations. But if your brand has grown to be bigger than just you, then you risk missing crucial aspects of the brand or skewing its purpose to your experience alone. We are looking for accuracy, clarity, specificity, and most importantly, something that will resonate with everyone on the brand team. Plus, it is easier and more fun to find your purpose if you share the burden of the exercise.

   Ideally your team would work through this exercise on a retreat. It doesn't have to be fancy. It could be a day-long off-site nearby, or even a half-day retreat. The key is that you are away from the office, without its interruptions and immersion in to-do list mode.

   Go in with an open mind. You can lead the retreat if

you feel you can dispassionately and without inhibiting employees' contributions. Often it is best to involve a third-party facilitator. This promotes openness and allows you to focus on hearing everyone's contributions. It also lets the facilitator probe areas of the conversation or comments that come up in a less inhibiting way.

The following questions are a starting place for your conversation. If you work with a facilitator, they might have a recommended approach. You might want to ask everyone to answer these questions in advance and bring their answers to the meeting, or collect them to consider and discuss with the group. Remember to contribute your answers as well.

Why did I/we start this business? (if applicable)
What attracted you to the company? (for employees)
What do we do?
For whom do we do it?
Why do we serve customers the way we do?
Why are we in this industry?
What image of our business do we want to convey?

The answers you collect may have relevance not only to your discussion on purpose, but also to the one on attributes.

4. **Determine the problem your brand solves.** Whether it is just you or your key team off-site, the next step is to talk about the problem your brand solves. In some cases, it will be the reason you started the business. It was a problem you ran into and couldn't find a solution to, so decided to create one yourself.

In other cases, especially when the business started as a

hobby, the question, "What problem does our brand solve?" will provide more insight than the reason you started the business. Your brand may have evolved from its origins based on customer needs and meaningful requests that have provided key revenue sources.

The problem you solve is not the provision of your particular service or product. "They need a hammer" is not a problem. The problem is the underlying reason that your customers seek you out. The problem you solve is your brand's contribution to the world. It should matter and be missed if your brand did not exist.

One way to uncover this is to talk about the different situations that precede your customer calling. What happens to prompt them to call you? What change has occurred for them?

Brainstorming and discussing all the conditions that prompt a request for your brand, and capturing them for all involved to see, will make it easier to look for themes that lead to the problem your brand solves. This is particularly true if it is not evident, or if it is hard to get beyond the "need for a product" thought.

5. **Identify the impact your brand has on your target audience.** How does your brand help them? Lasting and successful brands make the world a better place. How would the world be lacking if your brand wasn't there?

   Again, this needs to go deeper than, "We provide [insert your product or service here]." What does your brand enable your customers to do that they could not without it? How are they better off?

6. **Craft your brand purpose.** While I am not a fan of
   creation by committee, if your organization was big
   enough to need an off-site above, you might want to
   involve a few key employees in the crafting of your
   brand purpose. This is an intense endeavor and, again, I
   recommend getting off-site and setting smartphones aside
   to concentrate and escape daily distractions.

   Take the revelations you have from the process thus far,
   especially steps four (the contribution your brand makes)
   and five (the impact your brand has on your target audience),
   and develop your brand purpose together.

   Design your purpose to tap an emotion. Management
   consultant Graham Kenny said it best in his *Harvard Business
   Review* article, "Your Company's Purpose Is Not Its Mission,
   Vision or Values," "If you're crafting a purpose statement,
   my advice is this: To inspire your staff to do good work for
   you, find a way to express the organization's impact on the
   lives of customers, clients, students, patients — whomever
   you're trying to serve. Make them feel it."[16]

   The best brand purposes are clear, concise, easy to
   understand, easy to remember, and easy to execute. That
   translates to: less is more. The fewer words the better.

   A great format to use is optimist and organizational
   visionary Simon Sinek's formula from his "Find Your Why"
   course: To [contribution] so that [impact].[17]

   I like this because it encompasses not only how the brand
   contributes to the world, but the effect of its contribution.
   That clarity helps everyone on the brand team to understand
   what they are working toward.

   Use straightforward language. Start with the best
   descriptions of your brand's contribution and impact in the

formula, and then look to edit for clarity and brevity. You want to end with something that is easy to remember, easy to act on.

However, not every company uses this formula or format.

Examples of well-crafted purposes:

**Kellogg's:** "To create better days and a place at the table for everyone through our trusted food brands."
**Insurance Australia Group:** "To make your world a safer place."
**Nordstrom:** "To give customers the most compelling shopping experience possible."
**Sweetgreen:** "To inspire healthier communities by connecting people to real food."[18]

A brand purpose isn't something you spend an afternoon, a day, or a week on and then put in a drawer.

Your brand has to live its purpose for it to be true. Consistently adhering to your purpose reinforces your brand's identity, empowering employees to make good decisions that lead to brand growth and attracting customers who support your purpose and benefit from it.

Once your purpose is set:

1. **Evaluate your brand against its purpose.** How does each aspect of your business reflect your purpose? Where are you on course? Off course? Evaluate your brand offerings, operations, marketing, and resource allocations by whether they serve your purpose. You might need to make large and small changes.

2. **Write down goals for the business.** Prioritize your changes. You can't focus on everything at once, so look for the areas that will have the biggest impact, and work on those first. Or see if there is a logical succession to the changes and specify that.

   Write them down and use them as a guide to ensure your time, money, and efforts are taking you in the right direction. Use the SMART formula — Specific, Measurable, Achievable, Relevant, Time-bound — to craft your goals.

3. **Get to work on your goals.** Make the changes you need to make. Invest where you need to invest.

   A clear and meaningful purpose gets you halfway to solving your brand's identity crisis by telling the world what your brand wants to be. The second half answers the how-the-brand-wants-to-be-perceived question.

# Attributes Define Your Brand Personality

Attributes are the second half of the solution you need to solve your brand's identity crisis. Remember, Brand Identity = Purpose + Attributes.

Brand attributes are a set of three or four characteristics that answer the question of how your brand wants to be perceived, the second half of Erik Erikson's identity crisis solution. Your brand's defining attributes should be unique.

Do you know what your brand's defining attributes are?

My guess is that if your brand is having an identity crisis, either you don't know your brand attributes, or your team is emphasizing the wrong ones.

Well-chosen attributes:

- **Distinguish your brand from competitors.** This is the role that design and renegade attitude play for Apple, leading to sleekly crafted tech products and ads that encouraged people to "Think Different" or that mocked PCs as the stodgy establishment choice.

- **Appeal to your audience.** Defining attributes serve as touchpoints that your audience can relate to. They create a community for your brand. Harley-Davidson motorcycle owners revel in a rebellious, outlaw-like image. Tiffany & Co. shoppers self-identify with elegance, while Life is Good customers share an optimistic outlook.

- **Are genuine.** Life is Good's optimistic viewpoint comes naturally from their founders Bert and John Jacobs, whose mother asked them daily to, "Tell me something good."[19] Crocs' message of resilience resonates from a company that has faced hardship and offers shoes that have been vilified but have persevered.

- **Ring true with your audience's brand experience.** Crocs' claim on comfort works because customers have experienced it first-hand. Tiffany & Co. infuses all aspects of their shopping experience with elegance, from their well-appointed stores to the manner of their sales associates, to their robin's egg blue boxes with white bows.

- **Dovetail with your brand's aspirations.** Images form from repeated experiences, so your brand's day-one image — or even year-eight image — is unlikely to be the fullest expression of what your brand aspires to be. Defining brand attributes keep things moving in the direction toward that expression. Acceptance is an attribute Airbnb is always working toward to enable them to help anyone belong anywhere.

Collectively, your attributes define your brand personality. They determine the voice and tone of your communications and the ambiance of your workplace culture. They guide everything from the substance of your visual representations like logo, social media images, and advertising, to the manner in which your brand's customer service responds to inquiries and troubleshoots problems, as well as the way you deliver your products.

While Crocs' purpose centers on comfort, this is also one of their defining brand attributes, alongside fun and resilience.

We've already seen how Crocs' comfort attribute relates to their products, as well as their purpose as an accepting community that celebrates individuality and acknowledges life's difficulties.

Crocs infuse the brand with fun by the bright colors they offer, the upbeat nature of their communications, and the innovative and creative collaborations they engage in with designers and other partners. Crocs' first campaign, "Find Your Fun," did not fail because Crocs are not fun. It failed because fun was not the core of Crocs' proposition and did not resonate with customers as a reason for being.

Crocs embody resilience, from the brand's major business bouncebacks, to Croslite's ability to conform to a person's foot while keeping the integrity of the shoe, and the psychological aspect of being comfortable enough in one's own shoes to rebound from adversity.

Together, comfort, fun, and resilience create an image for Crocs that makes them unlike any other shoe brand.

## Know Thy Brand Self

Like your brand's purpose, your attributes are not just marketing fluff, but meaningful pillars of your brand. Knowing them well makes decision-making easier and keeps your brand on track.

Not knowing them can lead you astray.

This can happen even in a company of fewer than five people. Naomi Dunford learned this the hard way.

In 2006, after 10 years doing marketing and business development in Fortune 500 companies, Naomi decided to launch her own small business consulting firm by blogging.

As Naomi searched for advice on how to start her blog and run a business, she found there were websites that would advise on blogging and copywriting, but none that helped someone start a business. Websites that targeted small businesses were, "talking to the $10 million-$50 million companies, not someone making necklaces of clay."

The books Naomi found on starting a business focused on things like how to assemble a filing cabinet and advised founders to go to the Small Business Association and fill out forms. Nothing helped with the practical aspects of getting a small business up and running.

Meanwhile, the statistics on new business failure were staggering. Ten percent failed in the first year. Half of new businesses launched failed by year five.[20]

Savvy Naomi had found some white space and her purpose.

"White space" is an unfulfilled market need that no one is serving. "I wanted to help people create a business in a way that was less likely to fail," Naomi told me.

After initially trying to launch Itty Bitty Marketing locally, Naomi shifted her business online to Ittybiz.com in October 2007.

Naomi launched her business with her blog. Blogging was in its early days at that point. "Being lucid and articulate guaranteed success then,"[21] Naomi told me. In addition to her ability to articulate, she infused the blog with her personality. Which was not what you would expect from a Fortune 500 employee.

"I was always irreverent. I'd say a particular [profane] word and initially it would say zero on my blog reader count. Then the next day I would get an email that said, 'I can't believe you had the guts to say that.' I was the potty-mouthed marketer."

Naomi's gutsy language and straight talk about marketing for very small businesses won her legions of subscribers. They happily bought the hourly coaching and digital products Naomi offered. She also established an affiliate marketing revenue stream.

In a year she had a six-figure business.

Two years later, Naomi engaged email marketing and grew the business to over 1,000 customers. Ittybiz.com also employed her husband and a virtual assistant.

In the summer of 2010, two well-respected men in the industry offered Naomi advice. Both said if you are using foul language and looking like a screwup and making this kind of money, imagine how successful you would be if you cleaned up your act?

Feeling she should heed the advice of industry stalwarts, Naomi tamed her language and wrote "vanilla posts." Her business leveled off. Worse though, Naomi became bored with a business that she used to love. "It wasn't fun to be here any-more because I was boring. I was vanilla and beige and writing scared and doing the things you are supposed to do."

Stagnation threw Ittybiz.com and Naomi into a full-blown identity crisis.

While she knew her purpose was to help tiny businesses get started, she neglected to realize that her irreverence and pro-fanity were key brand attributes for Ittybiz.com. That tone had drawn in the subscribers who became customers. By following the advice of industry stalwarts, she had sidelined the character-istics that had distinguished Ittybiz.com and made it successful.

It took Naomi four years to figure out that something had gone wrong. "Two [more years] beyond that before I could comfort-ably pick up and write. I became really angry. I just realized I'd listened to bad advice, well-meaning advice from biased people. I had silenced myself."

In hindsight Naomi believes they meant well. "They see how they did things and think that's the way to do it." [22]

Naomi had let the fear of losing what she had built and some bad advice convince her that she should shed two of her defining brand attributes.

## Determining Your Brand Attributes

Now we roll up our sleeves to solve the second half of your brand's identity crisis by crafting your brand's personality — how you want it to be perceived.

Our aim is for you to land on three, or at most four, defining brand attributes, ones that distinguish you from your competi-tors. These traits will shape your brand's personality.

In order to ensure your brand's uniqueness, it is important to distinguish between category attributes that apply to all brands in an industry and attributes that are exclusive to an individual brand.

## Category Attributes vs Brand Attributes

To understand the difference between category and brand attributes, please think for a minute about Jerry Seinfeld. Or Chris Rock. Or Tina Fey.

Can you imagine if none of them were funny?

If you attended a stand-up comedy show and they were performing with a cold, you could excuse them for not being healthy. The show must go on.

If their outfit did not appeal to you, you could reason that style might not be their forte or that you have different tastes.

But if they weren't funny? That wouldn't fly. They are comedians.

People listen to comedians because they want to laugh. When you give comedians your time and attention, funny is the compensation you expect.

Comedians are in the business of funny. And if they weren't funny, you would have no interest in them.

Funny is a category attribute for them.

Category attributes are the characteristics that every player in your industry is expected to have. The aspects required to compete.

If you sell food, good taste is a category attribute for you. If you run a private school, individualized attention is a category attribute for you. If you sell racecars, fast is a category attribute for you. If you offer software-as-a-service, user friendliness is one of your category attributes (or at least it should be).

In each example, the category attribute is something every competitor needs to enter a prospect's consideration. That's how you know it is a category attribute.

Category attributes are the price of being in your industry. Defining brand attributes are on top of those, three or four that, in combination, are unique to your brand.

Your defining brand attributes distinguish you from your competitors.

Let's look again at comedians to see how their defining brand attributes work.

Jerry Seinfeld, considered the master of observational comedy, offers family-friendly humor in a laid-back manner.

George Carlin also practiced observational comedy, but was profane, fearless, and edgy.

Tiffany Haddish delivers her humor with unabashed candor, authenticity, and warmth.

Chris Rock highlights painful truths of black poverty, drug addiction, and race relations through his humor and often constructs cohesive arguments and insights through successive jokes.

Margaret Cho's crude and caustic humor addresses sexuality and race, Asian-American stereotypes, and other politically charged commentary.

Joan Rivers' unapologetic, blunt humor and searing wit made her a pioneer among female comedians.

Trevor Noah is an excellent storyteller who brings the audience along as he processes politics and the world around him with humor.

Tina Fey employs self-deprecating humor and a sardonic wit to comment on the world, all with a deadpan delivery.

Carrot Top has a mop of orange curls, goes for the cheap laugh, and employs props.

From each of their brand reputations, you know what to expect when you see any of these accomplished comedians.

Here's a table of their brand attributes:

| Comedian | Attribute 1 | Attribute 2 | Attribute 3 |
|---|---|---|---|
| Jerry Seinfeld | Observational comedy master | Family-friendly | Laid-back |
| George Carlin | Profane | Fearless | Edgy |
| Tiffany Haddish | Unabashed candor | Authentic | Warmth |
| Chris Rock | Painful truths | Race relations | Cohesive arguments/insights |
| Margaret Cho | Crude and caustic | Sexuality and race subjects | American-Asian stereotypes |
| Joan Rivers | Unapologetic/blunt | Searing wit | Female comedian pioneer |
| Trevor Noah | Storyteller | Process the world | Political humor |
| Tina Fey | Self-deprecating | Sardonic wit | Deadpan delivery |
| Carrot Top | Orange curls | Cheap laughs | Prop humor |

Nine comedians, each with distinct features. Audiences learned to associate these characteristics with each of them through their fidelity to their attributes and repeated exposure.

And it's not just stand-up comedy where you can observe these characteristics. The comedians remained true to them when they starred in television or internet shows, when they were interviewed, and in any public appearance they made.

Notice that these attributes come naturally from the comedian — the substance of their jokes and their delivery — as well as from their inherent characteristics.

These attributes ring true, but they might not be the ones

the comedians would have thought of or chosen themselves. It is hard to see defining attributes on yourself or your brand. Like the pediatrician who does not treat her own children, you are too close and too emotionally tied to the task to observe it objectively.

Your ultimate choice for your brand's attributes will be a mix of how its constituents view it and your aspirations for it.

Now that you understand the difference between category and brand attributes, you are ready to dive into the process of determining your brand's specific attributes to help it emerge from its identity crisis.

To start, you need to know how your employees, customers, vendors, distributors, and other partners think of your brand. How do you get to know what they think? You ask them.

## Collecting Attribute Input for Very Small Brands (Fewer Than 10 Employees)

If you are a very small operation, i.e. a one-person company or one-person fronted company, the attributes of your brand might be entwined with your personal attributes.

For a one-person organization, it might be enough to send your clients, colleagues, past colleagues, and collaborators (contractors you work with — even your accountant) an email asking them for the first three words that come to mind when they think of you. It can be a very short email. Here's what mine looked like:

*******

Subject: You Can Help in Only 90 Seconds!

Hi [person's name],

As part of my marketing efforts I'm working to understand how I come across. Please let me know the first three words that come to mind when you think of me.

Thanks so much for your help!

********

As a one-person company, you are the brand. That's why I have worded the email to ask about you. I would send this email to about 45-50 contacts. It's okay to include a few family members and friends, but make sure the majority of the contacts are professional. Not everyone will respond, but if you get at least 16-20 responses and can see a few attributes rise to the top when you tally the results, you may be set.

A similar approach will work for very small companies, those with no more than 10 employees. In that case you would reword the email to talk about working to understand how your *brand* comes across and ask for the first three words or phrases that come to mind when they think of it.

For in-person research, you might also want to ask what made them choose your brand, what they like about it or how they feel after making a purchase.

## Collecting Attribute Input for Larger Brands (More Than 10 Employees)

Brands with more than 10 employees will need a two-step process to ascertain their constituents' view of their attributes.

The first part of the process involves interviews with a few people in each of the brand's constituencies. These include employees and customers at a minimum, but can extend to vendors, distributors, sales reps (if not employees), and others who interact with your brand frequently.

These interviews should explore your constituents' image of your brand, including the first three words or phrases that come to mind and other questions to give you a good idea of how they think of your brand. It is important that the interviewer is someone to whom the interviewee feels free to speak candidly. Brands often engage a third-party researcher. Interviewees also need to be guaranteed anonymity for this to work well.

Twenty to 25 interviews are recommended. In general, you hope to see patterns and repetition among the responses. The goal of this research is to understand the breadth of answers that your brand draws.

Once you have the long list of attributes your constituents have articulated, you can conduct a survey among a much larger audience to see which of them rise to the top. The benefit of the first phase, and the reason it is necessary, is that now you can list the choices for your brand attributes with confidence that the list reflects reality. If you just picked the attributes yourself or with a few managers, you'd be force-feeding the responses and risking that the true perception of your brand is quite different, invalidating your research, and worse, mis-guiding your brand.

Respondents can check off the three or four attributes that first come to mind, which only takes a few seconds. Then you can offer them a chance to comment on why they chose those three or four. I recommend that, but it can result in a large data dump that someone will need to sift through and analyze.

Top three words or phrases that come to mind when you think of [your brand here]:

What makes you choose [phrase one]?
What makes you choose [phrase two]?
What makes you choose [phrase three]?

Like the first phase, survey respondents need to be able to respond anonymously to encourage candor. You'll want to send the survey to at least a few hundred brand constituents who have not participated in the first phase, and you should include customers, vendors, distributors, and outside sales reps — anyone who interacts with your brand. Your survey respondents should be a cross section of who you interact with.

## Choosing Your Brand Attributes

Once you and your team have the results of your attribute research, you should discuss where you see the brand going in the future. Based on your purpose, what are your aspirations for your brand's image? Are your aspirations a logical extension from where you are now? What attributes would your brand need to have to achieve these aspirations? Create a short list.

With the list of your top brand attributes from your research and your short list of aspirational attributes, finalize your brand's three or four defining attributes. Remember that these need to be authentic to resonate with your audience, so choosing all aspirational ones would risk your brand becoming unrecognizable. It's best to include only one aspirational attribute unless your brand is embarking upon a campaign to overcome an unfortunate reputation.

Though you've finished the process of choosing your brand attributes, your work with them is just beginning. Your team needs to infuse everything your brand does with these attributes. Apply your attributes to all your brand communication touchpoints: your website, packaging, emails, social media posts, marketing materials, and employee guides. This may involve much revision, but is crucial to establish and maintain your brand personality.

Like the comedians above, consistently using these attributes is how your brand will retain or evolve to the reputation you want.

## It's Important to Codify Your Brand's Identity

Once you have your brand identity defined — your purpose and your attributes — write them down, distribute them throughout your company, and keep them top of mind.

Naomi's experience with Ittybiz shows how easy it is to lose your way if you are not clear on both aspects of your brand's identity — its purpose and its defining attributes. Having your brand identity as a reference point helps you stay on track by giving you a litmus test for decisions to see if they are on brand.

A clear brand identity empowers you to:

- **Attract like-minded employees and customers.** A well-articulated brand identity helps your target audience see themselves in your brand and entices them to join your community. As Simon Sinek says, "People don't buy what you do, they buy why you do it."

- **Galvanize and align employees.** As your brand grows, so will its employee base. You can't be in all places at all times. Having a clear, easy-to-articulate, and memorable purpose inspires your employees, informs them of what they are working toward, and helps them make appropriate decisions for the brand to get there.

- **Allocate budgets with intention.** Rather than percentage increases or decreases for each department or project, your brand identity can put your initiatives in sharp relief, highlighting those that best serve your purpose and support your brand attributes. Funding the ones that will best move your brand forward can power growth and maximize your return on investment.

- **Choose the right product lines and new products.** Your offerings should support your brand purpose. Though Naomi's Ittybiz.com was essentially a business of one, knowing that she wanted to help very small businesses succeed led her to the right products and services to offer, which grew her business quickly.

- **Create the right marketing messages.** Rather than starting from scratch each time you launch a marketing effort, your purpose helps you develop meaningful messages that resonate with your customers and prospects over time. Your attributes help you express those messages in a voice and tone that your audience will relate to and that reinforces your brand image.

- **Assess opportunities.** If you are approached for a partnership, sponsorship or other opportunity to work with an entity, your brand identity will help you figure out if they are a good match. (You would also consider whether there is overlap in your target audience.)

Determining, writing out, and sharing your brand identity helps your organization make the right decision the first time and grow efficiently.

Your brand purpose and attributes serve as guideposts. Your brand's purpose is the first litmus test for new product ideas, the way you run your operations, marketing, and communications. Everything your brand does must serve its purpose.

Similarly, your brand attributes guide the manner in which your brand acts and communicates. They set the voice and tone of your communications. They help you assess whether a considered action — internal or external — would be in character for your brand.

Take a look at your current offerings and operations. Evaluate them against your purpose and attributes. Do they pass the test? If not, make changes until they do.

## Is Crocs Comfortable in Their New Identity?

So was Crocs' identity shift to comfort, fun, and resilience a temporary boost or a lasting change?

The brand had its best year yet in 2020, bringing in $1.38 billion in revenue, a 12 percent increase over 2019. They are projecting revenue to grow 20–25 percent in 2021.[23]

The "Come As You Are" campaign entered its fourth year in 2020 and continued to evolve its roster of global brand ambassadors, adding celebrities Priyanka Chopra Jonas (Indian actor, producer, global UNICEF ambassador) and Yang Mi (Chinese actor) to join 2019 ambassadors Zooey Deschanel (American actor), Kim Sejeong (South Korean singer and actor), and Suzu Hirose (Japanese actor). Collaborations with designers Christopher Kane, Balenciaga, Barneys New York, and Vera Bradley have emphasized Crocs as innovative and fun, as well as providing buzz value.

Crocs seems to have found their identity in comfort, allowing them to hit their stride.

## Avoid the Breakfast Club Bungle

*The Breakfast Club* is a movie about being honest with yourself about who you are. About authenticity winning over stereotypes.

Yet it succumbed to a trope that ruined my favorite character, the basket case, a girl named Allison Reynolds played by Ally Sheedy.

Allison is a mystery. Initially, she squeals instead of talking and bangs her head against a table. She does odd things like make a sandwich out of white bread, wheat bread, butter, Pixy Stix candy powder, and Cap'n Crunch cereal. She draws a picture of a bridge, then scratches her head wildly to make her dandruff fall on the paper so it looks like it is snowing.

Though she is looking for attention, she is unabashed and unapologetic about who she is.

I loved that.

But toward the end of the movie, the princess takes Allison into another room. In what is supposed to be an act of friendship, she gives Allison a makeover.

Allison emerges looking like . . . a princess-ized basket case.

She smiles, but is clearly uncomfortable in this new look. Worse yet, her makeover attracts the attention of the athlete, who kisses her.

After all the authenticity borne of sharing inner thoughts, why did the movie turn this genuine character into a fake? And why send the message that you need to conform to be attractive?

It's the one false move in a story that otherwise rocks.

To make sure your brand rocks, use your brand identity to stay on course and avoid false moves.

# Key Takeaways from Having an Identity Crisis

- Brand identity crises happen when there is lack of clarity in your organization about what your brand wants to be and how it wants to be perceived.

- What you want your brand to be is its purpose, how it will contribute to the world including the problem it will solve.

- How you want your brand to be perceived is the personality you want it to present to the world.

- Your brand's personality is defined by three or four unique attributes it exhibits in everything it does. Brand attributes differ from category attributes which every brand in your industry must have to compete.

- Brand identity = purpose + attributes.

- Your purpose differentiates your brand from competitors, attracts customers and employees, guides product and service offering decisions, and provides the basis for marketing the experience your audience can expect.

- Your brand attributes determine the voice and tone your audience experiences in every interaction with the brand, including internal communications with employees and external communications with everyone else.

# CHAPTER 4

# Running with the Wrong Crowd

## Signs Your Brand Is Running with the Wrong Crowd

A "Yes" response to two or more of the following questions signals that your brand may be running with the wrong crowd.

- Do you have trouble generating enough business to sustain your brand with your target audience?

- Do you need to keep rebuilding relationships with customers due to high turnover or frequent decision-maker changes?

- Do you find it difficult to generate repeat business with customers?

- Do your customers compel you to keep fighting for their business at every buying opportunity or renewal juncture, despite your relationship?

- Do any of your customers make unreasonable demands like 24/7 service or constantly renegotiate orders you thought were done?

- Do any of your customers monopolize your time with requests that require a disproportionate amount of attention relative to the revenue they generate?

- Do any of your customers press you to develop products or services specific to their needs but not appropriate for your brand?

- Do any of your customers make ethically questionable requests?

## The Company You Keep

On June 13, 1953, Gerald and Martha Dick welcomed their son Timothy into their Denver family. He would be one of six children.

Growing up, Timothy had a special relationship with his father, spending much time with him and mirroring his love for all things automotive.

At school, Tim's last name invited jeers and bullying. Tim developed a wit to deflect the insults classmates lobbed.

On the way home from a football game in 1964, Gerald Dick was killed by a drunk driver. Martha Dick moved her family to Detroit and eventually remarried.

Tim struggled in his teenage years, not caring about school except for shop class. After graduating high school, he began college at Central Michigan University then transferred to Western

Michigan University to earn a degree in Radio and Television Production.

He also began dealing narcotics on the side to make money.

After graduation in 1976, Tim Dick landed a job at an in-house advertising agency for a sporting goods store, but continued to deal drugs. On October 2, 1978, he was arrested at Kalamazoo Airport with 650 grams of cocaine — almost 1.5 pounds. He was released on bail.

While waiting for his court appearance, Tim tried doing stand-up comedy. He found some success, but his foray was cut short after he was sentenced to eight years in prison.

When he was paroled in 1981 after serving 28 months,[24] he faced a choice — continue to do business with the crowd that had landed him in prison or try to find a new audience to serve.

## Brands Can Run with the Wrong Crowd Too

To celebrate my 50th birthday, I threw myself a party. I love to dance, and looked to hire a DJ. Reviews on wedding website TheKnot.com raved about Spike Entertainment, and owner and DJ Spenser Brosseau. The site's reviewers mentioned how popular Spike Entertainment's photo booths and music choices had been.

When I went to Spike Entertainment's website though, the images and copy clearly targeted dances for high schools. I was confused, but I hired Spenser anyway. He did a great job.

It turns out I had caught Spike Entertainment in the midst of their brand adolescence.

Spike Entertainment began in 2006 when Spenser and a friend were in high school. They had been to several school dances and noticed that the music was not geared to their age group. They played around with the idea of becoming DJs to make a bit of money.

Their parents ignored their musings, but once they booked a gig at one of their high schools they actually had to commit.

"For the first couple of years it was more like a hobby," Spenser said. "Gigs came by word of mouth and were for people we knew. We spent the first year paying back what we'd spent on the equipment, and had some pocket change left over."[25] They hadn't studied the market and were undercharging for their services.

Spike Entertainment marketed their DJ services as specializing in school events, and only accepted school gigs. Their marketing pitch emanated from their chosen niche, wooing prospects to bypass large DJ companies with standard stock programs for a small company that did only school dances, knew what worked there, and tailored their services to please both the students and the administrators.

In Spenser's senior year he participated in a program run by DECA, a career and technical student organization that trains future leaders. His project with them qualified his business for their international competition. That was the moment Spenser decided to shift his DJ work from hobby status to a real business. His partner was already in college and was not interested in continuing with the business, so Spenser proceeded on his own.

Spenser planned to serve schools all over New England, envisioning them as regular customers requesting him year after year. But students graduated. Parent-teacher organizations frequently changed leadership. Faculty advisors rotated for school events. It was hard to capitalize on the relationships he built, as the players were constantly changing.

He continued pushing the school-dance-only niche until 2011

when he had a moment of reckoning that perhaps DJing dances for the school market would not be enough to sustain the business.

# The Wrong Audience Can Hold Your Brand Back

If you are a parent who has had teenagers, you have likely experienced situations where you wondered if some of your teen's friends were a bad influence or limiting their potential.

Adolescents seek friend groups who share a similar sensibility, like a shared passion (sport, hobby, music) or common disposition (political views, environmental concerns, antiestablishment thinking). Yet adolescents' lack of life experience makes it hard for them to judge whether those who share their sensibility are a good fit. Adolescents' desire to fit in can lead them to tolerate groups that get them in trouble, promote bad habits or belittle their individual interests in favor of groupthink or what is considered cool.

Similarly, brands in adolescence can sometimes have trouble recognizing when they are running with the wrong crowd.

When this happens, brands find they have chosen an audience that is too small — which limits their potential — or that their audience is stifling their growth due to excessive or inappropriate demands.

## When Your Target Market Is Too Small

Spenser's experience with Spike Entertainment is common. As Spenser found, the wrong crowd can mean targeting an audience that is not large enough to support your brand's growth. Spike Entertainment could not gain enough school clients to expand the business the way Spenser envisioned.

Brands in this position need to look for alternate markets that need their offerings and are big enough to allow room for growth over a period of years. Sometimes brands have to seek out these new markets. Other times they find them by chance.

For Lyft, the ridesharing company, the market shift came via technology.

Logan Green and John Zimmer launched Zimride in 2007, seeking to provide an alternative to car ownership to improve people's lives and prompt city designs to become people-centric instead of car-centric. Zimride's business focused on ridesharing for long-distance trips and on providing car-sharing services to college campuses.

In 2012, Green and Zimmer sponsored a hackathon project to figure out what Zimride would look like as a mobile app. Engineers built the app in three weeks. The company called the app Lyft. It launched on May 22, 2012.

A year later, Lyft was giving 30,000 rides per week and had raised $60 million in a funding round led by Andreessen Horowitz. Realizing Lyft offered greater potential to achieve their alternative-to-car-ownership goal, Green and Zimmer sold off Zimride's assets and focused on Lyft.[26]

# Dangers of Running with the Wrong Crowd: The Crowd Stifles Your Brand and Depletes You

Insufficient market size isn't the only problem you can have when your brand is running with the wrong crowd. Other burdens include:

- **Your market consists of "temporary friends."** If you find you are unable to generate repeat business from your target market, despite hard work and significant relationship-building time, this might indicate a mismatch. Spenser encountered this problem with the year-to-year turnover in decision-makers who hired DJs for school dances. Time spent relationship building was a sunk cost that yielded little when he needed to start a new relationship every year or when the customers he cultivated and served one year did not bother to call the next.

  It's one thing when your contacts move elsewhere in the industry and bring you a new customer. It's another thing when your existing customers have a revolving door requiring a disproportionate amount of time from you to build new relationships to retain their business.

- **Your brand is being bullied.** If there are customers you are serving who ask your brand to behave in a manner that makes you uncomfortable, it might be time to move on from those customers. This is especially true if your business is very small and these customers require a disproportionate amount of your time or cost you the opportunity of working with better customers.

  Ways in which your customers might be bullying your brand include demanding your attention during non-business hours. Or demanding that their requests be fulfilled in an unreasonably short amount of time or in a manner that causes you to shortchange other customers. In extreme cases, they might also request actions or forms of payment that are ethically questionable.

Bully customers can damage your brand by association, by the attention they require and the agita they cause, and by the things that serving them would require you to do and to ask of your employees. If a customer is bullying your brand, it is time to gently sever that relationship to create space for more positive and profitable customers.

- **Dominant customers monopolize your time.** These customers are not necessarily bullies, but require an inordinate amount of handholding, make excessive requests, and generally become black holes for your time. It is okay to have dominant customers when your relationship with them is healthy and when they pay in accordance with the service and attention they demand. But a customer who overloads your team with service requests without paying for them is a drain on your brand.

- **Your customer is trying to make your brand into something it is not.** Requests for products and services outside the purpose and scope of your brand should be referred elsewhere. If the customer repeats the requests often or complains of a lack of service in their desired area, you are better off opening up the resources spent serving them for a prospect who is a better fit.

Customer requests that are germane to your brand can be a great source of new product ideas. It's the ones that are clearly outside the realm of what your brand's purpose is that should be declined.

If these symptoms fit your brand, you might need to review your customer base and part ways from individual customers who are not a good fit, or find a new market.

## Separating from the Wrong Customers

If you have a diagnosis of running with the wrong crowd, your treatment will depend on a few things: whether your market is too small, whether you have a bad apple or two in your bale of customers, and the depth of your resources.

When your market is too small, the remedy is to shift your emphasis to a new, larger, and more profitable one. This might mean emphasizing the new market, but retaining some business from the original focus.

If your resources are very tight, you might need to shift them to the new market outright by gently letting customers know you are changing focus and referring them elsewhere. In reality, this shift is likely to happen over time as you gain traction in the new market. But once you make the commitment to the new market, all your marketing investments should go toward building that segment.

When individual customers are a bad fit or toxic, the antidote is to cut ties with them, but the task of separating is more delicate.

Toxic customers are not the same as challenging customers. Challenging customers pay for what they request and understand that fulfilling requests takes time. They might not be the best communicators, but they are invested in their requests and respond to your questions and outreach. Their requests might generate new opportunities for your brand and, ultimately, provide new product ideas. Just because they don't color within the lines of your brand doesn't make them bad.

Toxic customers don't value your work or your time, or they consider it less valuable than their own. They demand service at unreasonable times or within unreasonable timeframes. They try to bargain on prices or renegotiate set terms. They make you or your employees uncomfortable or reflect poorly on your brand with expletive-laden tirades, inappropriate jokes and behavior, or tantrums. They disappear often or at crucial times in your project timeline and make communication difficult. They constantly make you chase them for payment.

Any one of the behaviors above is toxic enough for you to consider terminating that relationship to make space for healthier and more profitable customers.

Once you have decided that terminating the relationship is the best course of action for your brand:

- **Remember that your goal is to part on amicable terms.** Just because your brand and this person were not a good fit does not mean they might not be a good fit elsewhere.

- **Choose the timing of your termination carefully for both of you.** For your brand, you might need to take your income into consideration and ensure you can meet your obligations. As for the customer, don't leave them in a bind. Your brand reputation will be affected by how you handle this, and helping them move forward is the professional thing to do. Decide in advance which competitor you believe will be able to help them.

- **Meet in person or by video chat.** Don't end the relationship via email or phone.

- **Explain the situation.** It's up to you whether to be candid about the issues in your relationship. You could begin with a phrase like, "I've noticed for a while that there have been some issues in our working relationship," and then tactfully mention some or all of them. If you go down this route, you may want to be prepared for the customer to offer to change behavior and then you will have to decide if you want to see if that works.

  If it is true that you are changing your focus by changing your target market, you can say that. Make it clear that your brand's circumstances mean you can no longer support their account.

- **Focus on their interests.** As you explain, incorporate what you know to be your customer's goals, and position your discussion and transition recommendations in their best interests.

- **Make it feel mutual** by using phrases like "not a good fit."

- **Be calm and professional.** Don't make it personal.

- **Set expectations** for what you will do to wrap up the business in process. Now is the time to refer them if you can. You probably took great care to bring them in as a customer. Take the same care to make their departure a positive experience if possible.

- **Don't say anything negative about the customer** to them or anyone else. You never know when circumstances will lead to a better connection for you, or when you might cross paths with their friends, family, and colleagues.

## Spike Entertainment's Gentle Pivot

Once Spenser realized the school-dance-DJ market would not generate enough business for his company on its own, he began keeping his eyes open for ways to expand his audience.

In around 2012, photo booths began showing up at events Spenser played, and quickly became a standard feature. A photo booth required major investment. Spenser studied the photo booth business and saw that low-ballers were going out of business, but that the better providers were charging meaningful fees.

Spenser then put together a business plan for a photo booth business and bought a booth. He kept that business separate and created a dedicated website for it. The photo booth business grew.

Diligently watching the numbers, Spenser noticed that he did fewer events in the year after getting the photo booth, but the average entertainment package he charged had almost doubled. The following year (2014), he doubled the number of events. Yet he still had to market hard to win the school events.

In addition to boosting revenues, the photo booth business

attracted some wedding clients. As Spenser ran photo booths at weddings, he studied their ins and outs. His confidence in serving the wedding market grew. Soon, new wedding clients asked to hire Spike Entertainment for DJ services as well as photo booth management. Spenser accepted these gigs instead of turning them down as he had in the past.

When he analyzed the business, Spenser saw that the wedding market provided greater customer loyalty and stronger word of mouth than schools did. Spenser prioritized the wedding market. Rave reviews on wedding resource websites TheKnot.com and weddingwire.com generated new leads.

By 2016 Spenser had tripled his business and felt established enough to hire a photo booth assistant to work with him at events instead of enlisting his parents or his girlfriend.

While school and community events were 90 percent of their gigs in the beginning, weddings now accounted for 75 percent of Spike Entertainment's business, with school events and birthday parties (including mine!) making up the rest.

Of his company's brand adolescence Spenser said, "Yes, we definitely had a brand adolescence, a couple of stages of it. When we first started out, we shot up and stayed steady for a while. But [to grow] we had to figure it out two or three times. We needed to grow into different markets and types of events."

Once you identify the new audience, shift your brand's attention to focus on them by aligning your message and all communication efforts toward them. Spenser has renamed the company Spike Events and revised his company website to have portals for weddings, parties and events, as well as photo booths. His main focus is clearly weddings, but event planners seeking services for school events, corporate events, and private functions can also find information easily.

# Finding the Right Customers

If your brand is running with the wrong crowd, you might be lucky and have new market opportunities present themselves, as Spenser's friends' weddings did for Spike Entertainment, and as Zimride's experiment with a mobile app led them to Lyft. If your brand needs a new and better market, and opportunities have not presented themselves, proactively find one.

If you had multiple target markets under consideration when you began, the ones you have not yet focused on might be candidates for a better primary target audience.

Begin by asking yourself these questions:

- Who do you want to help?
- What is the problem your brand solves?
- Who has the problem your brand solves?
- What are the circumstances that lead to a need for your brand?
- Who do you know has bought in the past?
- Who are your competitors' target markets?
- Where do you have existing relationships that you can leverage?
- What do you know about your brand and the problem it solves from past interactions with customers?

Ideally, this list of questions would lead you to brainstorm a list of potential target markets. If you have employees, you can involve them in the process. With your target market list, you want to be specific, but not limit yourself to demographic characteristics like age, gender, education level, and income. Dare to be more descriptive, like "working mother with two children in public school, one car, attending exercise classes twice a week, who likes to cook and eat healthy but does not have more than 30 minutes to get dinner on the table each evening." Or "event planner who needs budget-conscious swag to give out at the conference that looks classy but doesn't repeat what attendees typically receive." Or "couples getting married." Or "restaurants who want gluten-free dessert options for patrons to increase their average diner spend."

Next, determine your smallest viable market size.

In his book *This is Marketing*, marketing expert Seth Godin urges entrepreneurs and business owners to answer this question about your brand: "Who's it for?" Once you have identified your target, he encourages you to figure out the smallest viable audience for your idea by asking yourself, "What's the minimum number of people you would need to influence to make it worth the effort?"[27]

Translated to your brand's growth, this means, "What is the fewest number of customers you need to make your venture viable?" Be honest about the threshold number of customers you need to sustain your brand.

Targeting a new market is a major undertaking that can make or break your brand, so this is not a great time for trial and error. If you were running with the wrong crowd before, the last thing you want is to do it again!

Once you have your potential list of target markets and you know your smallest viable market size, take time to qualify your best choices through some research and analysis.

1. **Determine the market size for each new market candidate.** With so much information available online, chances are you can search to get an idea of the size of

each potential target market. While knowing the precise size would be nice, the hurdle we are looking for the market to clear needs to be large enough to support your brand given existing competition there.

For example, a Google search that Spenser might do for Spike Entertainment would be, "number of weddings in Massachusetts." The top listing for this search is a company called The Wedding Report which tracks and forecasts the number of weddings each year, as well as consumer trends in weddings. In 2019, there were 36,479 weddings in Massachusetts, with an average cost of $34,679.[28] Spenser has about 100 days each year he can do a gig, so he might determine that the market is large enough for him to try to find 100 events to work.

2. **What are the trends in the market?** In researching trends, you are looking for whether the market is growing, steady or shrinking, as well as insights that will help you be successful in the market. Again, using online search, you'll see that Statista reports that the rate of marriages performed in Massachusetts was 6.3 per thousand residents in 2018 and ranged from 5.5-5.9 in years 2006-2017.[29] While I could not pin down the number of DJs working in Massachusetts, I'm betting this would be a high enough rate to sustain Spike Entertainment for a while.

Through Knot.com I learned that the majority of weddings are black tie, so Spenser — who probably knows this already — would benefit from having a tuxedo. Most weddings occur in the summer and fall. Couples spend more on average to get married on Cape Cod than in Boston. On Cape Cod they spend an average of $1,561 for music, while in Boston the figure is

$1,485.[30] This kind of information helps Spenser understand the seasonality of his business and gives him an idea of the price range for his services (although this might include the cost of music during the wedding ceremony as well).

3. **Look at competitors.** Who do they target? What do the ones targeting your potential market charge? How long have they been in business? Can you set a price in the competitive ballpark and still be profitable?

4. **What are the circumstances in which this market seeks your product or service?** For Spenser this is easy — couples planning a wedding. The circumstances prompting a need for your product or service might be less obvious, and you might need to talk to customers and conduct market research to learn more about them and how often they occur.

5. **How feasible is it for your brand to service this market?** Feasibility issues can include the amount of funding needed to operate at a high enough level to serve the market, the equipment needed, the processes involved in delivering your product or service, and the geographical proximity to the audience.

6. **What existing relationships or leads do you have in the market?** Spenser's friends provided his first requests for a wedding DJ service and then gave him a potent source of referrals and testimonials to help him grow. Do you have relationships that would give your brand a running start and insight into this market?

7. **Would this market be a good source of repeat business and/or referrals?** If you install air conditioners, the cycle between one installation and the next might be 20 years. But if your industry involves shorter or frequent sales cycles, would this market support repeat business and referrals? We saw how the school market changed its decision-makers year-to-year, making it a tough sell for Spenser. But newlyweds happy with their DJ service were quick to recommend them to their engaged friends. Choosing a market where referrals and repeat business are easy will lower your customer acquisition cost and make generating business easier.

## Tim Dick Retools His Career

In prison, Tim's wit garnered him a reputation for being able to make even the toughest guards and inmates laugh.

After being paroled, Tim worked at an ad agency by day and did stand-up comedy by night. He honed a macho persona and did some commercials for Mr. Goodwrench.

His stand-up career gained momentum. In 1990, Tim's "Men Are Pigs" routine, which focused on men's love for hardware, was made into a Showtime television special. It caught the ear of then-Disney CEO Michael Eisner and then-Disney Studio Chairman Jeffrey Katzenberg, who tried to book Tim for television adaptations of the movies *Turner & Hooch* and *Dead Poets Society*.

Instead, Tim persuaded them to create a new sitcom based on his routine.

When Tim did his first talk show, the producers said they did not feel comfortable flashing his real name on screen. They feared people would think he made it up to be funny.

And that was the moment Timothy Alan Dick became Tim Allen.

The Disney-funded sitcom was *Home Improvement,* which ran from 1991–1999 and earned him a People's Choice Award for Favorite Male Performer in a New TV series in 1992, and Favorite Male TV Performer from 1993–1999. He also garnered an Emmy nomination in 1993 and a Golden Globe Award for Best Actor in a TV Series in 1995.

Tim Allen's other roles include the voice of Buzz Lightyear in all four *Toy Story* movies, a starring role in *Galaxy Quest* and a reprised lead role for the *Santa Clause* movie franchise.

Tim Allen's pivot to an audience large enough to sustain him in a service that did not get him arrested is still getting him roles today.

# Key Takeaways from Running with the Wrong Crowd

- Brands are running with the wrong crowd when their target market is too small for them to grow or when they serve customers who are a bad fit or toxic.

- A key sign of running with the wrong crowd is that your organization is investing significant time in serving a customer without receiving a commensurate benefit in sales, referrals or new expertise.

- When the market is too small, it is important to qualify a new market for the brand to grow by ensuring it is a good fit and meets the brand's smallest viable market size requirement.

- When a customer is a bad fit or toxic, the brand should sever its relationship with the customer, but do so delicately to avoid leaving the customer in a lurch and to protect the brand's reputation. Even severance is a brand experience.

- Leaving insufficient markets and mismatched customers frees resources for serving markets and customers who are a better fit for the brand and will help it thrive through long-term relationships and repeat business.

# CHAPTER 5

# Acting Self-Centered

## Signs Your Brand Might Be Self-Centered

Now to the delicate question of whether your brand in adolescence is self-centered. Assessing the answer requires frank responses to the following questions. If you answer "Yes" to two or more, your brand might be self-centered.

- Does your organization have recurring internal, customer-facing or partner-facing problems?

- Do you observe situations where employees are pointing fingers or deflecting responsibility?

- Do situations arise where you find yourself or your employees remarking on how customers are wrong?

- When customers complain, do you and your employees look to placate them to make the complaint go away?

- Do you have a set of requirements or values you ask of your employees, but from which you consider yourself exempt?

- Do employees represent your brand in a way that makes you cringe?

- Do you work to counter negative employee or customer reviews?

## You Should Be Grateful to Me

Early in the movie *The Social Network*, Erica Albright (Rooney Mara) and Mark Zuckerberg (Jesse Eisenberg) are dating and meet at a bar. Erica is a student at Boston University (BU). Mark is a student at Harvard University.

Mark pines to join one of Harvard's elite clubs because he believes it will introduce him to worthy people and lead him to a better life. That goal monopolizes his thoughts and efforts.

Erica calls him on his obsession, but he characterizes his mentality as motivated, not obsessed. Mark tells Erica that she ought to be more supportive because if he got admitted he would take her to club events and she would get to meet people she would not otherwise encounter.

Erica's patience with Mark's "motivation" runs out and she excuses herself to study. Mark claims she does not need to study because she goes to BU.

Exasperated with Mark's condescension, disdain and self-serving behavior, Erica tells him,

"You are probably going to be a very successful computer

person. But you're going to go through life thinking that girls don't like you because you're a nerd. And I want you to know, from the bottom of my heart, that that won't be true. It'll be because you're an asshole."

Mark's anger and frustration with Erica prompt him to go back to his dorm and vent on the internet about her, although he harbors hope of not losing her. It also prompts him to launch the social network "Facemash," a precursor to his creation of Facebook.

## Growth Spurts Catapulted Facebook's Size Ahead of Its Maturity

Facebook has become such a fixture in people's lives that it is hard to remember Mark Zuckerberg founded the social medium in a Harvard dorm in 2004, and that it has only been open to the public since September 2006.

The platform experienced a meteoric rise from one million monthly active users (MAU) and $382,000 in revenue in 2004, to 845 million MAUs and $3.7 billion in revenue in 2011 to 2.80 billion MAUs and $84.169 billion in revenue in 2020.

Like a gangly 16 year old who sprouted four inches in each of the last three years, Facebook has both sought growth and struggled to keep up with it. And like that adolescent, the brand's size and allure has masked some of its immature behavior.

CEO Zuckerberg acknowledged this point in an interview with *The New York Times* on March 21, 2018:

"Mr. Zuckerberg said that the company's efforts to safeguard its platform from bad behavior . . . were an important part of a larger transformation at the company, which has had to adjust from its roots as a social network for college students into a powerful global information hub."[31]

*The New York Times* also reported that Sheryl Sandberg, Facebook's COO, has been trying to appease lawmakers by saying that, "the company was grappling earnestly with the consequences of its extraordinary growth."[32]

Efforts to cope included staffing up. Facebook has been hiring at a breakneck pace for the past four years, largely to get more eyes reviewing what is posted. Facebook employed 6,818 people by the end of March 2014.[33] At the end of 2020, that number had multiplied more than eightfold to 58,604.[34]

Zuckerberg and Sandberg would have you believe that Facebook as a brand is like Tom Hanks' 13-year-old character Josh Baskin in the movie *Big*, whose wish to be big is granted by a Zoltar fortune teller machine, transforming him suddenly into the body of 35-year-old man.

Revelations via company emails and newspaper investigations suggest the truth is closer to Reese Witherspoon's ruthlessly ambitious Tracy Flick in the movie *Election*, whose sweet appearance belies her tactics to win.

# The Rebellious and Self-Centered Brand in Adolescence

In June 2017, Facebook changed their brand mission from "to make the world more open and connected" to "to give people the power to build community and bring the world closer together." Zuckerberg explained that the reason for the change was not only to get a diverse set of opinions heard, but "to build enough common ground so we can all make progress together." A lofty, admirable, idealistic goal.

Zuckerberg is famously competitive and ambitious, prone to act now and think later. Facebook's five core values reflect his nature:[35]

☐ **Be bold:** "We encourage everyone to make bold decisions, even if that means being wrong some of the time."

☐ **Focus on impact:** "We expect everyone at Facebook to be good at finding the biggest problems to work on."

☐ **Move fast:** "We're less afraid of making mistakes than we are of losing opportunities by moving too slowly."

☐ **Be open:** "Informed people make better decisions and have a greater impact, which is why we work hard to make sure everyone at Facebook has access to as much information about the company as possible."

☐ **Build social value:** "Facebook was created to make the world more open and connected, not just to build a company. We expect everyone at Facebook to focus every day on how to build real value for the world in everything they do."

Zuckerberg's ambitions have fueled the company's meteoric rise, but they have also occluded and downplayed serious issues that have come back to haunt the company.

Data breaches. Fake accounts. Fake news. Election meddling. Hate campaigns.

Violence incited through posts.

Under Zuckerberg's leadership, Facebook has proven to be a self-centered and rebellious brand in adolescence.

The brand's business success seems to have fueled in its leaders the idea that they can pursue their interests for the brand without worrying about the consequences. As news of data breaches, fake news and election meddling emerged, Facebook's reaction mirrored that of a rebellious teenager:

- **Oblivious to the problem:** The data breaches, fake news and election meddling were news to them. They seemed initially unaware that it was happening.

- **Denial:** Immediately following the US 2016 Presidential Election, critics blamed Facebook's spread of fake news as an undue influence in the outcome. Zuckerberg's initial reaction was, "I think that's a pretty crazy idea. Voters make decisions based on their lived experiences."[36]

- **Blame shifting:** In Zuckerberg's February 2017 letter, he blamed "sensationalism in the media" for moving people from "balanced nuanced options toward polarized extremes."[37] When summoned to testify before the Senate Intelligence Committee in September 2019, the company lobbied to have Google representatives show up as well.

- **Rationalization:** After British lawmakers released Facebook emails discussing the idea of selling users' data, the company spokesperson said the emails were only internal conversation and, "We were trying to figure out how to build a sustainable business."[38]

- **Attempt to mitigate disciplinary action:** In an interview with CNN on March 21, 2018, Laurie Segall asked

Zuckerberg why Facebook shouldn't be regulated. His response was that they should be regulated but that, "the question is more, what is the right regulation?"[39] When pressed about the right regulation, however, Zuckerberg expounded on the need for ad transparency and said nothing about data management and privacy.

☐ **Failure to see the consequences of their actions:** Facebook delegates the policing of their platform to moderators who are charged with enforcing the company's 27-page community guidelines. Many are third-party contractors. Most are underpaid, overworked, and inadequately supported. Moderating flagged content often means viewing hundreds of grisly and repulsive images each day. Moderators need the same kind of support that first responders receive. Other organizations asking employees to view objectionable and illegal content provide four to six months of training compared to Facebook's four weeks.[40] They also require regular counseling and provide additional access to psychological support.

Due to their size and market position, Facebook is an extreme example of a self-centered brand in adolescence, largely because they have gotten away with this behavior for 16 years and have achieved a market capitalization of over half a trillion dollars.

But most self-centered brands in adolescence don't achieve a fraction of this success.

## The Segway Saga

Have you ever ridden a Segway?

The original battery-powered Segway Human Transporter (HT), now known as the Segway Personal Transporter (PT), used five gyroscopes connected to a computer system that gauged the rider's center of gravity more than 100 times per second to "self-balance," enabling the rider to travel upright at 12 miles per hour.

Inventor Dean Kamen envisioned his Segway as a change agent for urban planning, relieving traffic congestion and offering a zero-emission, fossil-fuel-free solution for people to use to commute and on the job. His intentions were good.

But his vision was grandiose and created in his mind with no supporting research and analysis. He believed entities like police departments, the post office, FedEx, and Amazon would flood his factory with orders. Consumers would clamor for their own.

Announcing the Segway PT on *Good Morning America* on December 3, 2001, Kamen predicted hundreds of thousands of sales, and then leased a 77,000-foot manufacturing facility in Manchester, New Hampshire to meet that demand.

Kamen's team lobbied state legislatures and municipalities all over the US to permit Segways on the sidewalk. By the end of 2002, 32 states and the District of Columbia had changed their laws to accommodate them.

Critics who questioned the Segway's safety were told the company would offer four hours of training to purchasers. Kamen's inner circle could not fathom how someone could try the Segway and not become enamored with it.

After the initial excitement fanned by Jay Leno, Sting, and

Russell Crowe tooling around on Segways on *The Tonight Show*, reality set in. FedEx passed. The US Postal Service bought 40 Segways for a trial, but after mail carriers found the PTs did not save time and were impractical in the rain, they passed too. Disney was an early customer, but ordered dozens of Segways, not hundreds.

## Cost and Lack of Consumer Testing Hobbles the PT

Segway delayed the consumer launch of the PT to work out training and safety issues and to establish it as a serious product by virtue of its corporate and professional sales. Yet out of fear of being beaten to market by a competitor, the company had developed and continued to develop the PT in secret. All testing took place within the confines of Segway's offices, with the shades down and blinds closed.

Though none of the training and safety issues had been solved and professional sales foundered, the Segway PT became available to consumers on Amazon in November 2002. It weighed 80 pounds, traveled 11 miles on one battery charge and cost $4,950. The high cost inhibited purchases.

Finally, in 2003, early employee Matt Gelbwaks conducted a study in Celebration, Florida, to understand how people used the PTs. The company sold the scooters to 100 residents at a steep discount. Even at the reduced cost, nearly all the participants stopped using them within a year. Gelbwaks learned then that the significantly nerdy image associated with Segway precluded their social acceptance.

A lack of consumer testing had hidden the cost and image issues from the company. It also masked safety issues, which became apparent in a high-profile way.

US President George W. Bush fell off a Segway in 2003. Piers Morgan made fun of him, but then broke three ribs falling off one himself in 2007. Ironically, James Heselden, who bought the Segway company from Dean Kamen in December 2009, died after accidentally riding one off a 30-foot cliff near the River Wharfe in Yorkshire, England, in September 2010.

Local emergency rooms fielded scores of adults and children injured in Segway accidents, prompting them to be banned on roads and sidewalks in the United Kingdom, San Francisco, and parts of Barcelona and Prague among many other municipalities. In 2004, Disney prohibited park visitors from using them.

Advances such as anti-tip technology, more comfortable foot mats, and gliding lights for better visibility have improved safety and user experience. But the brand's laser focus on distribution and getting sidewalk permission made many customers and municipalities feel it did not prioritize safety and did not have their best interests at heart.

While engineers could improve the safety of the PT, little was done to reduce the cost and, therefore, the price. Jim Norrod, Segway's CEO from 2005 to 2009, told CNN, "A lot of people said our products were too expensive, they were too high-priced. Yeah, they were. You know why? I needed the money to run the company."[41]

By the time Roger Brown bought the company in 2013 for $9 million, the 14-year-old brand had become a punchline, the company was in disarray, and they had yet to show a profit.

Brown did not have the same allegiance to the costly technology and save-the-world view as longtime employees did, and quickly moved the brand to profitability. He saw the potential with tour companies using PTs, but he still failed to research broader consumer trends and attitudes toward scooters.

On Brown's watch, Segway did get the US International Trade Commission to investigate companies suspected of infringing on their patents for self-balancing technology. Ninebot was listed on Segway's complaint. When approached about the patent infringement, Ninebot quickly offered to buy the company, paying $75 million for it on April 15, 2015.

Paying $9 million in 2013 and reaping $75 million in 2015 — quite the return on investment, right?

Maybe. But Ninebot took their existing knowledge of the personal transport category and immediately capitalized on Segway's brand recognition and technology by launching several Segway-branded scooters and other products priced at $1,000 or less. These scooter variations sold better and faster than the PTs. It helped that companies like Uber, Lyft, Lime, and Bird were offering scooters for rent.

"If I would've had the vision of Bird or Lime," Brown said. "Segway would have been worth $10 billion."[42]

# Dangers of Self-Centered Brands: Wasted Money, Uncoordinated Brand Efforts, and Legal Problems

Self-centered brands focus on their own advancement. Brand growth reigns supreme and garners respect, prompting the brand's culture to reward growth and ignore other measures of success and impact, such as community improvement or talent development.

Growth is obsessively measured and reviewed on a short-term basis. Lack of growth is an emergency; strong growth catapults those responsible for it to greater power and compensation.

A brand's culture can be ruled and distorted by laser focus on growth and the accompanying metrics. Metrics like number of monthly users or amount of advertising at Facebook. Metrics like number of municipalities approving Segway's PT for sidewalks.

Employees at every rank realize that demonstrating their contribution to growth is the only way they can advance in stature and compensation. These motivators often encourage individual employee action over teamwork.

Some employees will develop their own agenda to show their contribution, regardless of what their department or the organization as a whole is trying to achieve. Anxious to have their name attached to growth-producing measures, they will allocate their budgets and efforts to what they can claim as success. Managers who shift to this modus operandi lose the trust of their employees, who feel the manager will not have their back if they do not go along. Unaligned teams and uncoordinated operations lead to wasted money and time, as not all of the efforts will succeed and some may contradict others.

Other employees will find the pressure to show growth in the short term or working solely to make the boss look good is a toxic environment, and they will leave or diminish their work efforts. This decreases productivity and creates high turnover, which in turn raises talent acquisition costs.

For the employees who remain, as Simon Sinek explains in his book *The Infinite Game*, the lack of trust among employees and teams, and the focus on results, might lead brand team members to begin rationalizing unethical behavior to succeed in performance metrics that are rewarded. Repeated over time, this rationalization becomes ingrained in their thinking to the point that they no longer see themselves as doing something wrong. Sinek calls this "ethical fading" — behavior people normally know is wrong, but persuade themselves is the right thing to do because the compensation system and corporate goals "force" them to do it. They blame the system to justify their actions.[43]

For example: sharing access to personal data to grow a business and generate revenues which, in turn, support your stock price (looking at you Facebook).

Or allowing your product to be developed without safety testing or consumer feedback, in the case of Segway. Kamen's enthusiasm for the product and fear it would be pirated cast a spell over the company such that no employee would challenge him on those product development aspects, which led to user injuries and deaths.

Most detrimentally, employees' and customers' experiences with a self-centered brand will often lead them to mistrust the brand and to terminate their relationship with it. Trust lost is exceptionally hard to regain. People who leave your brand community in frustration, anger or disgust are unlikely to give it a second chance.

Facebook experienced this backlash in March 2018 after news broke of the Cambridge Analytica scandal, unleashing the #DeleteFacebook movement. A Pew Center survey in late spring 2018 showed that 26 percent of Facebook users said they had deleted their accounts.[44]

While most brands are unlikely to experience such a large and public customer departure, a self-centered brand will lose customers and see its customer acquisition costs increase.

## Values Keep Your Brand on Course

The antidote to free a self-centered brand from its egocentric focus is a definition — or in Facebook's case, redefinition — of the brand's values.

As we saw in Chapter 2, your brand's purpose provides the reason you are in business, and is a key component of your brand's identity. Values give your brand a soul and collectively act as a behavioral guide to achieving your identity. Choosing the wrong values is like operating with faulty GPS: they won't take you where you want to go. Or they will, but they get you into questionable areas on the way.

Some companies have paid lip service to brand values or created them as an exercise and then put them aside. As you can see from the way Segway and Facebook have gone astray, values — spelled out or not — define the culture and have a real effect on it. Management signals what a brand's values are by the way they operate and the behavior they reward.

If management's values in practice differ from what they have professed on paper, employees notice. The days of believing you could tell your employees one thing and have a separate set of customer-facing values are over. Review websites like Glassdoor .com, Indeed.com, and Vault.com, alongside social media like Facebook, Twitter, and LinkedIn have provided ample opportunities for employees to share their experiences and feelings about your company. It also means that you no longer control everything the public sees about your company, and that anything that happens there could become public.

At the same time, brands living exemplary values attract and retain top talent. Engaged employees lead to happier environments, higher productivity, longer tenures, less churn, and better brand performance. Desirable values also attract like-minded customers.

Your values come from your leadership and your brand community. Your values are a mix of the way your brand community conducts itself and your aspirations for that conduct.

## Segway's New Owner Puts Values to Work

Segway-Ninebot's first listed value now reads, "Centered on the user's value." The other three are, "Strivers-oriented," "Driven by innovation," and "Results-oriented."

The company is clear about its commitment to safety, and has helped develop electric battery safety standards with the American Society of Testing and Materials (ASTM) and the American National Standards Institute (ANSI) which are used internationally. The company has also worked with the Association Française de Normalisation (AFNOR), the national standardization institute for France, and is working with China and the US to develop mutually recognized standards for the self-balancing vehicle product category.

When scooter-sharing company Lime blamed Segway for electric batteries that were catching fire on one of Segway's scooters, Segway responded that the issue lay with Lime's maintenance practices. Segway-Ninebot will not let safety issues go unanswered. They understand safety is a scooter category value they must uphold as a market leader with a self-reported 80 percent of the shared scooters in operation.[45]

Ultimately, Segway did contribute to the revolution in electronic transport that Dean Kamen envisioned. But Segway's values of perfectionism, change-the-world evangelism, and municipality blessing precluded both the progress of their goal and the ability of the brand's founding crew (and early owners) to profit from it.

# Declaring Your Brand Values

Brand values are a collective set of beliefs. Done right, they should articulate what you and the people you want to attract to your brand believe and guide how you act on the brand's behalf. Values define your company culture and, as founder of Zappos Tony Hsieh said, "Your culture is your brand."[46]

Having a clear set of values not only communicates how you want your employees to act, but also helps ensure a consistent and high-quality customer experience. Your brand's value set keeps it community-minded and makes it clear self-centered behavior is not welcome.

For brands in adolescence, the process of defining brand values is less about deciding and creating them and more about declaring the ones that have come to define the best of your organization.

## Involve Your Employees

Unless you are a company of one, you don't have to craft your brand values alone. In fact, you shouldn't. Determining values, like choosing attributes, is a collective exercise and should begin with as many members of your organization as possible. It's especially important to include long-serving, well-regarded employees and those you consider important for your brand's future. Employee involvement increases your chances of choosing values that resonate with your brand community.

Not involving employees and superimposing values on your brand organization risks them not resonating with your brand community and backfiring. Inauthentic values can hurt a brand's reputation as much as genuine ones help.

Brand values must be specific to your brand and designed to create the workplace environment you seek and the customer experience you want to deliver.

For this reason, I advocate that brand teams start from scratch and avoid using a predetermined list of values. What makes your brand values unique is in part the wording that arises from your employees. It is likely to be more specific, meaningful, and colorful if the words or phrases arise naturally from discussion.

Here are the values from five brands to give you an idea of how specific and unique successful value descriptions are:

# Five Companies and Their Values

| Life is Good | Zillow | Ikea | Zappos | Zen Planner |
|---|---|---|---|---|
| Boston, MA | Seattle, WA | Delft, Netherlands | Las Vegas, NV | Denver, CO |
| Apparel manufacturer | Real estate information | Ready-to-assemble furniture, homewares retailer | Online retailer | Fitness business software |
| 200 employees | 4,336 employees | 211,000 employees | 1,500+ employees | 101 employees |
| | | | | |
| Authenticity | Act with integrity | Togetherness | Deliver WOW through service | O: Outstanding service |
| Gratitude | Move fast, think big | Caring for people and planet | Embrace and drive change | H: Honor |
| Creativity | Own it | Cost-consciousness | Create fun and a little weirdness | A: Anticipate |
| Love | Zillow Group is a team sport | Simplicity | Be adventurous, creative, and open-minded | N: Nimble |
| Courage | Turn on the lights | Renew and improve | Pursue growth and learning | A: Active |
| Compassion | Winning is fun | Different with a meaning | Build open and honest relationships with communication | |
| Simplicity | | Give and take responsibility | Build a positive team and family spirit | OHANA means family |
| Humor | | Lead by example | Do more with less | |
| Openness | | | Be passionate and determined | |
| Fun | | | Be humble | |

A few sentences typically follow each value to explain and expand on it to promote common understanding.

## Aim for 5-10 Values

How many values should you have? Zappos has 10. Zillow has six. Ikea has eight. Life is Good has 10. Zen Planner has five.

As you can see, there is no set number. Most successful brands have between five and 10 values. My advice is to see where the process takes you and how many values you need to articulate a vision of the culture you have or wish to create. Aim for five to 10 values, but don't feel constrained by that range. Know, though, that in order for the values to be lived, they need to be remembered and reinforced.

## The Values Declaration Process

Your brand in adolescence has been operating for some time, so this process will help reveal your values and position your brand to be deliberate about them. Your final list of values is likely to be a combination of pre-existing values with possibly one or two aspirational ones, especially if the brand is at a juncture in its evolution.

I recommend a seven-step process. Seven might seem like a lot, but they facilitate the process and ensure diligence and perspective.

A quick note before we dive in. I'm giving you detailed instructions for each of the seven steps to make them as clear as I can for you to execute. It's a lot to absorb. If you are reading the whole book through right now, you may want to skim each step to get the gist of it and then return if and when you need to implement the process.

Okay, here we go. The seven steps are:

1. Observation gathering
2. Employee input and discussion
3. Grouping for themes
4. Filtering and prioritizing
5. Crafting the list
6. Testing for resonance
7. Disseminating and embodying — ongoing

As business owner and leader, you need to be involved in this process. You can lead the process if you can do so dispassionately and objectively.

I recommend getting an outside facilitator. This frees you to absorb more of what is being said without having to manage the session. It will also help you keep an open mind as you listen to what your employees have to say. If you can afford to hire a professional, that's great. If not, try to enlist someone who is objective, energetic, and can make people feel at ease.

For this process, you will need large sticky pads and small sticky notes in three different colors. I recommend the 3"x3" size.

## 1. Observation Gathering for Context and Perspective

Gathering observations brings a real-world view into your process and helps you avoid formulating values in a vacuum. You can think of this as setting the scene. We want observations of what customers think of your brand and of your current company culture.

Seek customer input from any consumer research your company has conducted, from unsolicited customer testimonials and from customer service department raves. Mine positive reviews and social media comments. You are looking for what customers like about your brand when it is at its best. Capture comments verbatim and assemble a collection of them to share with employees.

Take whatever customer input you find and have someone analyze it to look for themes. Have that person capture verbatim comments on sticky notes of a particular color, one comment per note. If there is an obvious theme, label the note with that theme.

Observing current company culture also helps provide context for values discussion, but this is optional. If you don't have the time or resources for this, company culture can just come up during discussion in the early part of the process.

The best approach I have seen for assessing company culture upfront comes from brand expert Denise Lee Yohn in her book *Fusion: How Integrating Brand and Culture Powers the World's Greatest Companies*. She suggests using an ethnographic approach she calls "a culture audit." Yohn recommends getting a cross-functional team to conduct the audit. If your company is small, the team could just be two people or even the outside facilitator.

The culture audit starts with an anthropological take on your office, a walk through your brand's work environment, and noting any posters, sayings or visuals in your employees' workspaces and congregating areas. Collect any signs or symbols. It is worthwhile to chat with employees to see if the visible evidence is true to the environment, aspirational, or hypocritical.

The audit then moves to study company communications, compensation structure, office location and layout, rituals the company conducts (for example, recognition ceremonies or annual events), and artifacts (items your company keeps, displays, distributes). The team is looking for indications of your brand culture in all of these areas — whether it is informal or formal, individual-performance or team-oriented, competitive or collaborative, modern or old-fashioned, industry-leading/following or disruptive.[47]

## 2. Employee Input and Discussion

The primary driver of your values idea generation should come from members of your organization. After all, they are the ones who have been acting on the brand's behalf. Their insider views will both enlighten you and provide context for the values creation.

I recommend providing each employee with a list of questions in advance and a pad of sticky notes. Use a different color than the one you used to capture the customer comments and themes. Ask employees to record each value they think of on an individual sticky note and to bring them to the employee discussion session.

Questions that can help values discovery include:

1. What are our company's greatest strengths?
2. What is important to you about our customer relationships?

3. What do we stand for?
4. What do we value most?
5. What personal values do you bring to work and uphold even when not rewarded for them?
6. What does your work convey about you?
7. What values does our company stand for when we face obstacles or difficult situations?
8. What do our customers believe about us?
9. What are the 3-5 most important behaviors we should expect from every employee (including you, the business owner)?

On the day of the employee input and discussion session, meet somewhere you won't be disturbed and have everyone focus by separating from all electronic devices.

Open the meeting by sharing the results of your observation gathering, as that could prompt more values discovery and discussion. Encourage employees to continue to capture their values ideas on sticky notes as they occur to them.

Consider one other beginning activity to inspire creativity and help the group get ready to discuss your company's values. One great upfront activity that Spotify used as they began their values determination process was to have employees share stories of their favorite moments at work, success stories, and things that make them proud to work there.

Other fun exercises that add creativity and dimension to this initial part of the process include:

1. **Brand eulogy.** Have employees write a eulogy for the company. What would people say about the brand when it is gone?

2. **Brand birth announcement.** Ask employees to write a birth announcement for the company. What would people wish for the brand?

3. **Tap other industries.** Have each person mention one or two favorite brands in other categories and say what they love about them.

Encourage sharing and discussion of the values that emerge. If your company is small and you have fewer than six people participating, you can do this as one group. If you have more than six people, break into groups of 3-5 people. Research shows people are more likely to participate and speak up in groups of that size.[48]

Have someone take notes to capture the words used to describe each value during the discussion. Take care to get the exact wording down. It's okay if the wording is controversial or unconventional for business; capturing the true sentiment is the goal right now. Wordsmithing at this time risks losing the original sentiment. Resist the urge.

## 3. Grouping for Themes

Reconvene the group if you divided into subgroups and share the values that emerged and any insights that came up. Once discussion has bubbled up some themes, write them on large sticky pad pages, using one page per theme and post them. Have employees place the sticky note with values they wrote that align with the theme on the relevant page. Grouping can take some time and is likely to prompt conversation about which comments belong with which themes.

Have someone place the customer input sticky notes on the relevant theme and add new themes if applicable.

If you conducted a company culture audit, discuss those results with the group. Which observations ring true? Discard any inaccurate observations. Take the ones that ring true, record them on a different color sticky note, and apply them to the relevant theme.

Have the group review the themes. If the process has worked well, you should have a visual idea of which values are most prevalent.

While your ultimate goal is five to 10 values, it's okay if you have more than that for now. This is a great place to end the large group meeting or put a break in the process. It is good idea to start the next step another day so that the team can begin rested and fresh, and have had some time to ponder the themes and values.

## 4. Filtering and Prioritizing

If you did steps two and three with a large group, formulate a smaller group to do the rest of the work. This smaller team should be well-regarded employees who have a handle on the culture and who represent different areas of the company.

In this third phase, the team will filter the themes and values that emerged through some reality checks and begin prioritizing the values with an eye toward culling the list. Cull with care and avoid premature judgment.

Discussion questions that lead into the third phase — filtering — include:

- What themes emerge as supported by all three areas — employee input, customer input and, if conducted, culture audit?

- Are there different takes on the same theme? If so, combine those.
- Do any fall away as not really true?
- Do any fall away from low support?
- Are there insights that make the themes more specific and ring truer? Capture those.

Once you have discarded any themes that do not hold up to scrutiny, take stock of the remaining ones. If you have many more than 10, direct the conversation to see which ones are strongest and double-check that there is no duplication. Remember, you are looking for the values that most define your brand culture and make it unique.

Now prioritize the list based on the values with the strongest evidence and support. It is less important to identify a specific 1, 2, 3, 4, 5 . . . right now than to take another pass at which values most represent the brand. Once prioritized, take another look to see if any of the lowest listed values naturally fall out of contention.

At the end of your filtering and prioritizing stage, aim for at most 10 distinct values themes unless your group feels strongly that your brand merits more.

## 5. Crafting the List

This is the step where the representative group will draft your values list.

It helps to have someone take notes in this session to capture the discussions. In this phase, your goal will be to craft the list of values as well as some brief explanation of each to qualify it and make its meaning clear. Having employees' actual wording helps make the values unique, memorable, and resonant.

Discuss the themes that made the cut in the filtering and prioritizing round one by one. Delve into them to see if there are comments or wording that capture the essence of the theme. These can form the basis of your value statement and the supporting sentence or two you will use to illuminate and clearly convey what the value means to your organization.

Aim for wording that gets your employees excited or impassioned. Again, wording that originated among them promotes understanding, ownership, and commitment.

Do any of the values jump out as spot-on for your brand culture or a leading value? Put them first on the list.

You may need more than one session to craft your list. When your draft is done, you will have 5-10 values with a brief description to follow explaining or elaborating on what it means.

## 6. Testing for Resonance

Values guide behavior: behaviors create culture. Values should help employees make decisions, initiate actions, and guide responses to tough situations and opportunities. There is a direct line between the values you endorse and the culture you nurture. This is not an exercise you will redo frequently; this is hopefully a one-time setting of guidelines. As such, you need to vet each value to see if it contributes meaningfully to the culture.

After some time to let the values draft list sit (overnight or longer), reconvene your representative team and work with them through these questions to evaluate and tweak your values list.

- Does each value describe a distinct aspect of your culture? Clarify if necessary, to avoid overlap or duplication.

- Does each value correspond to at least one desired behavior?
- Does each value help you make decisions?
- Do the values collectively depict the culture you want for the brand?
- Do the values work together as a set? Ensure none of them conflicts with another or would lead to a confusing situation.
- Do they feel right?
- Do your chosen values mesh with your behavior and the behavior of your leadership team? Everyone needs to embrace the brand values and live them for them to be effective. That includes being able to recognize and call out hypocrisy.
- Are the values meaningful? Edit out any fluff or superficial stuff that snuck in.
- Can your company uphold these values under duress, such as competitive threats, downsizing, a product recall or other crisis?
- Are you willing to defend these values unconditionally?
- Do these values permeate every area of your organization?
- Can you see yourself defending these same values two or three decades from now?

The ultimate test will come when upholding your brand values is not the easy route.

Edit and tweak your values draft list until you have a final list that feels right and has the buy-in of your representative group.

# 7. Disseminating and embodying – ongoing

Values determination is an iterative process, but once you have arrived at the final set of values that works well for your organization, your last step is to declare them before shifting into education and embodiment mode.

While the road to this point has been long, the only thing that saves your brand from self-centeredness is the adoption and consistent practice of the values you worked so hard to define. Don't skimp here!

Find fun and creative ways to introduce the values list to your organization, and do it more than once, in more than one way. People need repeated exposure to learn and remember.

Ideas to roll out the new values:

- Have a kickoff party or event to launch them. Create swag or mementos that employees can keep. Announce the values yourself, say what they mean to you, and make their importance to you clear.

- Create fun events to promote your brand values and discuss them. You could have themed events based on the values. If one of your values is about following through, have an obstacle course event. If creativity is a value, initiate an annual employee talent show. If gratitude is a value, write your employees thank-you notes.

- Post your brand values on your website and let the world know your commitment.

- Issue a press release.

- As you roll out new policies and programs to support your values, take the opportunity to have an event to celebrate this.

Ideas to keep your brand values ever-present in people's minds:

- Post your brand values in employee common spaces, both physical ones like break rooms and digital ones like Slack groups.

- Include them in employee handbooks.

- Talk about your brand values when recruiting, and again in the orientation process. Include them in recruitment and new hire materials.

- Hire people who embody your values. Pass on those who don't, even if they have great performance track records.

- Let go of employees who don't adhere to your brand values. This one is tough, but as we mentioned earlier, living strong values means upholding them in tough situations. Allowing a consistent violator to stay among the ranks weakens the values and sends a message that you aren't serious about them. Ultimately, it weakens your brand.

- Encourage and enable living the values with deliberate events, like the talent show mentioned above, employee appreciation events, or community service outings.

- Equip employees to live the values. If gratitude is a value, let employees handwrite thank-you notes to customers. Or allow them time to give back to the community in a manner of their choosing.

- Align your policies and procedures with your values. If life balance is a value, revisit your time-off policies to align them with true life balance. Ensure employees are compensated in a manner consistent with your values.

- Whenever you address your employees or send out an announcement, call out your values when it's relevant to the topic.

- Recognize and reward employees for living the values. This reminds your team of your values and assures them of your continued commitment.

- Promote your values on your website. In addition to their presence from the launch, talk about them on your blog and other relevant pages.

This does not mean if you discover a flaw in your values you can't fix it — of course you can and should. If the process has worked well though, you'll either have them right or very close.

Most of all, practice your brand values, live them, and endorse them every chance you get. Employees take their cue from you.

## Consequences Speak to the Self-Centered Brand in Adolescence

Facebook has yet to make major changes to their values or show they can stem the tide of abuse to their platform. What happens to self-centered brands that don't self-correct, like Ninebot is doing with Segway?

Self-centeredness is a one-way relationship. Parents addressing self-centeredness stop giving in to the adolescent's demands. They require mutuality before they will reinstate the adolescent's desired action. You want the car Saturday night? Kindly take out the garbage as I asked you earlier and you may have it.

Self-centered adolescents benefit from strong parental guidance, but so far no one has stepped into that role for Facebook. Not Facebook's board. Not the US Government. Not foreign governments.

That may be changing. On July 24, 2019, the US Federal Trade Commission (FTC) fined Facebook $5 billion for deceiving users about their ability to control the privacy of their personal data. The FTC also mandated additional oversight, personnel, and regular reporting on Facebook to improve their data handling and privacy protections.

In addition, the FTC opened an antitrust investigation on Facebook in June 2019. The US Department of Justice also initiated a huge antitrust investigation into Facebook, Google, Apple, and Amazon in July 2019.

But with all this trouble you may be thinking: is Facebook stalled or plateauing? Isn't that a criterion for brand adolescence?

Yes. And their stall has come in the form of user base decline.

According to Edison Research's Infinite Dial Study, Facebook usage declined from 67 percent of the US population aged 12 and over in 2017 to 62 percent in 2018 and then 61 percent in 2019. Use of Facebook's Instagram app grew from 34 percent in 2017 to 36 percent in 2018 and then 39 percent in 2019, so that shift may explain some of the decline. Still, Facebook as a brand is losing users.

Facebook may not feel the consequences of that loss, both because of the increase in Instagram users and possible participation in their WhatsApp messaging platform, but also because revenues continue to grow. Revenues more than doubled from $39.42 billion in 2017 to $84.17 billion in 2020.

The Federal Trade Commission's $5 billion fine on Facebook will hardly put a dent in their revenues. However, if the FTC or Department of Justice's antitrust investigations result in undoing Facebook's acquisition of Instagram or WhatsApp, the brand will begin to feel the sting.

Meanwhile, Facebook continues to operate within their self-centered values and has made clear company-wide that these are the values that are rewarded.

If Facebook was serious about changing, they would acknowledge that real change has to come from within. If Facebook was serious about developing a more mutual relationship with their customers and constituents, they would change their values to reflect what they are giving lip service to in public. Prioritizing privacy. Safeguarding data. Building common ground.

Instead, like an adolescent who tries to negotiate favorable parental limits, Facebook is asking for government regulations for the global technology industry that they already meet.[49] Zuckerberg wants the brand to re-establish credibility by showing it is adhering to rules and answering to someone with authority but without real change.

At the end of *The Social Network*, one of Mark's lawyers, Marylin Delpy, advises him that he will need to settle the court cases facing him. She adds, "You're not an asshole, Mark. You're just trying so hard to be."

The movie closes as Mark sends a friend request to Erica Albright and keeps refreshing the page to see if she has accepted, but gets no response.

The message is clear: self-centered actions burn bridges, cost friendships, and cause loneliness.

# Key Takeaways from Acting Self-Centered

- Brands act self-centered when their values dictate and reward self-centered behavior.

- A brand's values are the set of beliefs that guide the actions of its leaders and employees.

- Brand values define the company culture. They may be explicitly stated or implicitly understood from the goals leaders set and the actions they reward via accolades, promotions or raises.

- Correcting self-centered brand-in-adolescence behavior begins with defining or redefining values to reflect how you want everyone associated with the brand to act on its behalf.

- To remedy self-centered brand-in-adolescence behavior, brand values must be lived consistently by everyone associated with the brand, including you, the leader.

- The true test of brand values comes when they guide a difficult decision, like recalling a product, adjusting policies for customers or employees in light of a pandemic or letting go of a productive employee who does not adhere to the values.

# CHAPTER 6

# Suffering from FOMO and Trying Too Hard to Fit In

## Signs Your Brand Is Suffering from Fear of Missing Out (FOMO) and Trying Too Hard to Fit In

If you answer "Yes" to two or more of the following questions, FOMO may be holding your brand back.

- Has your product portfolio ballooned? Do you have a nagging feeling you should prune some products, but feel reluctant to eliminate any?

- Is your brand team afraid to take a stand on what you will and will not offer? Are you afraid to not carry everything your competitors carry?

- Does your brand team say yes to customer requests even if they don't play to your brand's strengths? Do you rationalize that pleasing the customer justifies venturing outside your comfort zone and taking a hit on costs?

- Do your marketing communications list all the same benefits or product features as your competitors?

- Have you tried to emulate your competitors' marketing and found none of it grows your brand?

- Does your marketing just seem to follow the latest craze or new medium with little to show for it?

## Fit In or Miss Out

Sixteen-year-old Cady Heron had been homeschooled all her life until she arrived at North Shore High School for her junior year. She was smart, kind, and a social clean slate.

Her naïveté got her in trouble with teachers and classmates repeatedly on her first day.

Janis Ian, a tough black-rimmed-eyed girl, took pity on Cady and taught her the lay of the land, clique-wise. Most of all, Janis and her friend Damian cautioned her to watch out for the Plastics, a clique of three polished rich girls including the Queen Bee of the school, Regina George.

But the Plastics took an interest in Cady, invited her to sit with them for lunch and to go shopping with them. Janis did not hold this against Cady, but hatched a plan to destroy Regina and to use Cady's acceptance into the clique to execute it.

So begins the 2004 film *Mean Girls*.

Once Cady (Lindsay Lohan) had been accepted into the

Plastics, she felt pressure to stay in the group. That meant conforming to their rules and playing along with all their activities, like criticizing aspects of their bodies. Cady was perpetually afraid of falling out of grace with them, especially Regina (Rachel McAdams). She began wearing more makeup. She wore pink on Wednesdays per their decree. She adopted a snooty attitude.

Her efforts to fit in worked. But then Cady fell for Regina's boyfriend Aaron Samuels (Jonathan Bennett). Her ploys to win Aaron from Regina began with her feigning ignorance in math and asking him to tutor her, and ratcheted up to her finally divulging that Regina cheated on him.

Regina and Aaron split up. Cady had a party, and invited Aaron and a few friends over.

The whole junior class found out about the party and showed up, including Regina who raged, "She thinks she's gonna have a party and not invite me? Who does she think she is?"

Why would an ultra-cool Queen Bee rage about not being invited to a party? Her rage comes from fear, fear of missing out. Aka FOMO.

## FOMO: The Endless Hamster Wheel of Fear

Have you heard of FOMO? People of all age groups experience it, but it's most common in people under 30. A 2013 study defined FOMO as "the uneasy and sometimes all-consuming feeling that you're missing out — that your peers are doing, in the know about, or in possession of more or something better than you."[50]

A 2015 study in Australia found that one in two teens suffered from FOMO.[51]

Teens who are affected by FOMO constantly watch what others are doing and posting, say yes to events they don't have time for, spend money on things they can't afford, and feel endless anxiety — all in the name of trying to keep up with everyone else. In the quest for always making the best choice or attending the best event, FOMO sufferers sometimes find themselves in analysis paralysis — unable to make a decision for fear of making the wrong one.

And like the human version of FOMO, the behavior of trying to be all things to all people can paralyze your brand. Instead of keeping the brand open to all opportunities as many owners think, it actually stunts growth.

## A Confectionary Dream Becomes a Retail Nightmare

When The Chocolate Truffle, a shop in Woburn, Massachusetts, went up for sale in 2003, Erin Calvo-Bacci saw an opportunity to shift from supporting corporate brands to building equity in her own business. Erin had worked in business development for several years, including stints for Haven's Candies and Fanny Farmer. She also enjoyed making lollipops and other confections. With two daughters under three years old at home, Erin and her husband Carlo Bacci bought The Chocolate Truffle.

Erin soon learned that business development and running a retail shop were radically different. "We took over a week before Thanksgiving. I lost 14 pounds in three weeks. It was baptism by fire."[52]

The prior owners had been sourcing product from more than 10 different vendors, all of varying quality, and one whose product was infested. The store's original location did not lend itself to foot traffic. Erin and her husband also inherited a large staff who had been indulging customers by gift wrapping items bought elsewhere for free.

Operationally, Erin had to clean house and to get sourcing under control.

Erin and Carlo bought a building in Reading, Massachusetts in 2006 and moved The Chocolate Truffle there.

To solve the excessive and inconsistent supplier issue, Erin and Carlo took over production themselves by buying a local manufacturer and consolidating all production in Swampscott. They launched a wholesale division under the name Bacci Chocolate Design. In addition to filling The Chocolate Truffle shelves, they also sold product to the competition.

## Throwing Spaghetti at the Wall

To grow the business, they opened two more locations for The Chocolate Truffle. "We were known for handmade truffles, but people were still coming in for other products from the store's history. I felt like our brand was having an identity crisis."

Moreover, the two businesses combined were still not making money. Erin tried all sorts of marketing and new product efforts to become profitable.

"We were throwing a lot of spaghetti at the wall and hoping it would stick. We did a rebrand of the website. We partnered with *Phantom Gourmet* (a Massachusetts TV show featuring culinary retailers and restaurants) to get exposure. We did cross promotions. St. Germaine makes an elderflower liqueur; we made an elderflower truffle. We enlisted a marketing company and helped promote two movies, including *Sex and the City 2*. We tried to do cupcakes, but those are so perishable — it was a nightmare."

So many random efforts and attempts to provide all the products requested nearly killed the business. "In 2009 we were a wink away from dead," Erin said.[53]

## The Secret Sauce to Brand Success: Focus

Have you ever dreamed your brand could become the Amazon of your industry?

Today you can buy almost anything on Amazon, but the brand gained its reputation selling books. Jeff Bezos' vision was for an "everything store," but he knew he had to make a name for his company with one product first before he could expand.

In other words, he needed a niche.

How big can you get on a niche? Isn't that limiting? Well in 1997, two years after launching, the company had 256 employees and $60 million in sales. It reached $203 million in sales in 1998, still just selling books.

That's a pretty good running start. Amazon isn't the only behemoth that began that way. Whole Foods made their name selling organic foods when few others were. ESPN dedicated themselves to sports 24 hours a day when few thought sports alone could sustain a media channel.

A niche isn't always a single product category. There are many ways to define a niche, and we'll talk more about that later. Right now, the point is this: a well-chosen niche is the best way to differentiate your brand and position it for growth.

Yet many business owners shy away from establishing a niche for fear that it will limit their brand. They dismiss this notion because they believe appealing to a narrower slice of their perceived audience will reduce both revenues and the size of their customer base.

Others choose a niche, but never establish it because when it comes time to pare non-niche-conforming offerings from inventory, their FOMO surfaces and they can't commit.

# Dangers of FOMO:
# Rudderless Marketing, Analysis Paralysis, and Lack of Differentiation

Business owners suffering from FOMO fail to see the ways in which it hurts their brand.

Like Cady Heron in *Mean Girls*, brands that try to please everyone find it hard to consistently please anyone. They launch a presence on every new social media platform because they think their competitors are doing it, stretching their marketing staff and budget too thin to have any meaningful effect. They cater to every customer request, even when those requests require investments that might be a net loss for the company. They stock low-demand inventory because the idea of missing a sale, however rare, is unbearable.

FOMO prevents the brand from ever saying no to a presented opportunity. With no specific focus or strategy, the brand team has no guidelines on what the brand should and should not attempt. Trying to please everyone and be everywhere is exhausting. Chasing every opportunity achieves less than focusing on the best markets for the brand, and wastes time, money, and resources too. It hinders brand growth.

This was what was happening at The Chocolate Truffle, what Erin Calvo-Bacci meant by "throwing spaghetti at the wall." It nearly drove the business into the ground.

For other brands, FOMO ironically results in their missing out on many things.

Few marketing budgets can accommodate all marketing channels and product opportunities. When the brand team is forced to make a choice to allocate resources, the process of choosing becomes excruciating. Fear of making the wrong choice, of missing out, fuels endless analysis. No one wants to be the one who did not explore the angle that would have led to the right decision.

And no one wants to be the one responsible for the wrong decision. In the face of this fear, some teams fall prey to analysis paralysis and opt not to decide. The pain of not deciding is less than the fear of making the wrong decision.

In this case, fear prevents anything from happening. No opportunity ventured. No chance for growth.

Brands suffering from FOMO also feel compelled to match every competitor's products, features, and benefits. To not do so seems like taking the brand out of contention.

The opposite is true.

The compulsion to mirror your competitors makes your brand less competitive. If your offering is exactly like your competitors', why should customers choose your brand? Mimicking everything your competitors do robs your brand of its differentiation. Or at least buries it.

Meaningful differentiation is what helps customers remember your brand and inspires them to choose it. In the long run, your brand can differentiate itself by the experiences it delivers, but those experiences have to happen to get to that point. When you are initially competing, offering something unique is the only way to stand out. It is the only way to establish a foothold in the marketplace that no other brand can claim.

To differentiate, your brand needs to focus. A niche helps by providing natural guidelines for your marketing, for your offerings, and for whom your brand will target. Analyses have a particular end goal, enable decision-making, and no longer paralyze the brand team.

A brand flourishes when it finds its niche and commits to it.

# Busting the Niche Myth

Focusing on a niche helps you build a strong reputation and become the go-to brand for your audience. Business owners shy away from niches, though, for fear that they will limit the brand's potential. This is not true.

There are three major reasons you should develop a niche if you haven't already, especially if your brand is struggling or on a plateau.

First because brands that succeed do so because they become known for something and niches speed that process. With a niche, your brand stands for something specific. Having a niche allows you to speak directly and specifically to your target market and bond with them. It frees your brand to focus on one area to develop expertise and depth beyond your competitors.

Second, niches position your brand well for repeat business. The expertise your brand develops makes it the first, and often only, stop for your target audience. Getting to know your audience's needs and wants in depth means you can often develop companion and additional products to serve them. Repeat business is much cheaper to acquire than new business. It is also less expensive to service and more likely to prompt referrals.

Third, niches work in your favor because developing a specialty creates a halo of competence around your brand, giving it credibility that it can expand on later.

Sometimes it takes the accidental discovery of a meaningful niche to lead a brand there. That's what happened to Barbara and Arielle Freedman with their baked goods business.

## Barbara Begins by Baking Brownies

In 1995, Barbara took over a friend's small brownie business in Amesbury, Massachusetts. Barbara loved to bake and switched the business to her own brownie recipe, figuring she would bring in a little extra income.

In the summer of 1998, The Flatbread Company was launching their restaurant chain with a first location in Amesbury. The owners found Barbara's brownies at a farm stand. On a handshake, they struck a deal for Barbara to provide brownies and desserts for their restaurant. The Flatbread Company grew over time to 18 locations, growing Barbara's business in tandem. Flatbread Company employees knew her as Barbara Brownie, so that's what Barbara named her company when it came time to incorporate.

One day Barbara made a delivery to a Flatbread Company restaurant and noticed a table where the parents and some children were enjoying her brownies, but a gluten-free child was not.

That bothered Barbara.

Barbara's mission was to make something where no one ever felt deprived. She thought everybody should be able to enjoy a good brownie. The vision of that child excluded from dessert haunted her.

Barbara brought her daughter Arielle into the business in 2008. In addition to producing the regular brownies and desserts in their product line, they began formulating a gluten-free brownie recipe with the same high-quality ingredients including unsalted butter, all-natural vanilla, and top-grade chocolate chips.

After much experimenting, the Free-At-Last gluten-free brownie made its debut in 2009. Gluten-free diners would be free at last to enjoy a brownie for dessert alongside their family and friends.

## Gluten-Free Gets Going

Using Barbara's vision of that deprived child as inspiration, she and Arielle set a goal of enabling gluten-free diners to enjoy dessert worry-free. To remove the possibility of a mix-up between their regular and gluten-free brownies, Barbara and Arielle made the Free-At-Last brownies circular. The Flatbread Company hesitated when presented with a circular brownie, but soon appreciated the operational ease that they had baked in. No risk of serving the wrong brownie and making a diner ill.

In considering the quality and service of their products, Barbara and Arielle do more than provide a gluten-free dessert. They say to gluten-free diners, "I see you. You matter to me. Here is something you can enjoy."

The success of the Free-At-Last chocolate brownie and the joy it brought to the underserved gluten-free population spurred Barbara and Arielle to broaden their offerings to include additional brownie flavors, cookies, and pound cakes. They found their mission in serving the gluten-free population.

Barbara, Barbara's husband Ron, and Arielle decided that gluten-free was where they wanted to focus the business. Dedicated to the strict guidelines qualifying gluten-free products, they knew they had to get production out of their Hampton, New Hampshire home kitchen. They found a small space in town in 2014, designated it Gluten Free Territory, and launched the gluten-free business as a separate entity under that name. Reinvesting their baked goods earnings, they purchased ovens, triple sinks, and pans on Craigslist.

While Barbara and Arielle still produce regular brownies, cookies, and cakes at their original kitchen, marketing funds and efforts focus entirely on Gluten Free Territory, and include trade shows like Nourished Festival in Worcester, Massachusetts (formerly The Gluten Free & Allergen Friendly Expo). Over time, the team has invested in professional photography, new labels, and a new website.

In addition to restaurants, Gluten Free Territory sells to local retailers and schools and is available for purchase online. The business is growing.

Are Barbara and Arielle worried about serving fewer people by focusing on Gluten Free Territory? No. The gluten-free niche, while small relative to the total baked goods category, is growing fast.

According to Grand View Research, the global gluten-free products market was valued at $21.61 billion in 2019 and North America accounted for 40.61 percent of the revenue share. The global market is projected to grow at a compound annual growth rate of 9.2 percent from 2020 to 2027.

Bakery products dominate the gluten-free market. Global Market Insights reported that the global gluten-free bakery products market size totaled $7.4 billion in 2018.

## Aim Narrow to Grow Big

Does it matter to Barbara, Arielle, and Ron how big the global market is? No. They see a local need and ample room to grow. And they are growing.

Savvy entrepreneurs look for gaps and underserved areas in the marketplace which they call "white space." They know that being first and prominent in an uncontested space with a demonstrated need reduces the risk of investment. Great tasting gluten-free desserts — there are plenty of unappetizing ones — were and are a fertile white space for the Gluten Free Territory team.

Any competitor can make regular brownies and desserts. Gluten Free Territory's delicious gluten-free desserts set them apart and allow them to own more market share. Their proprietary recipes mean that competitors are hard-pressed to match their performance. Niches are a recipe for brand differentiation and growth. By focusing their efforts on Gluten Free Territory, they are becoming the go-to provider for gluten-free bakery items in New Hampshire, Massachusetts, Maine, Rhode Island, and Connecticut.

## How Narrow Should Your Niche Be?

I can see the trepidation in your eyes. What if I make my niche too narrow? Won't that hurt my brand? It is true that you need sufficient market demand to support your brand.

But it is rare that a brand defines its niche too narrowly. It is way more common for brands to cheat their niche by extending themselves into other markets or products that don't fit. Cheating undermines the benefits of a niche by not establishing the niche sufficiently, or at all. It is the niche that helps your brand rise above competitors.

Don't be afraid to go narrow. How narrow? Narrow enough so that your audience feels your brand is the exact solution they seek.

Even the Golf Channel is a billion-dollar business. Who knew? For me, the Golf Channel would be a sleep aid. But my husband is riveted.

Know also that there is leeway to course correct your niche if you go too narrow at the onset.

Airbnb, another multibillion-dollar business, began in an overly narrow niche. The business was conceived as creative lodging to fill the overflow demand that hotels could not accommodate in a city hosting a large conference. The founders targeted conferences like South by Southwest and the 2008 Democratic National Convention.

How did they figure out the need to broaden the niche? They quickly found that frequency of conferences large enough to create demand for overflow housing was not enough to support the business. At the same time, existing customers asked to use the service on vacation or for business in cities where there was no conference. It wasn't long before the founders set up a test in New York City to see how non-conference related rentals would work. Clearly the test succeeded.

The risk of an overly narrow niche is small, especially for brands in adolescence that have already survived the start-up stage, but the benefits to a well-defined niche abound.

## Benefits of Defining Your Brand's Niche

In addition to positioning your brand as the go-to in its category, a niche makes your life as a business owner easier and fuels growth.

1. **A niche allows you to focus.** You have limited resources — time, money, effort, staff. A niche channels your resources in one meaningful direction. This creates a powerful synergy and helps align your organization toward the same goal.

2. **The focus of a niche brings deeper understanding of your brand's audience and of your niche.** Understanding your target audience better than anyone else gives you an advantage over competitors because you can serve them better by leveraging that knowledge in what your brand offers and how you deliver those offerings. Superior knowledge of your niche, and continuous learning there, makes it difficult for a newcomer to challenge you.

3. **Your niche guides your key marketing messages.** No more reinventing the wheel each time you and your team decide to advertise, post on social media, or exhibit at a trade show. Your in-depth knowledge of your audience means you can communicate with them and tell your brand story in a way that resonates more than your competitors. You can market your brand with confidence.

4. **Your niche guides your product offerings and new product decisions.** Your niche becomes the litmus test of what product offerings to keep and what to pare to make room and free resources for new offerings. Filtering new product ideas through your niche lens helps you pursue the ones most likely to appeal to your target market.

5. **Your niche makes it easier for your target audience to recognize your brand as its go-to solution.** In your marketing, sales, and customer service, your niche has your brand team displaying its knowledge of your audience and speaking their language. As Mary Adams, founder of the Exit Planning Exchange and Smarter-Companies said to me, "The more specific you are about

what your niche is, the easier it is for people to work with you."

6. **Your niche helps your audience remember and recommend your brand.** Fidelity to, and success in, your niche pairs your brand name with that niche and brings it to the tip of your customers' tongues whenever someone asks for a referral for what you offer.

Still worried that a niche will constrict your brand? Take a look at Google. Valued at $323.6 billion in 2020,[54] they are still working their niche. (Few actually call them Alphabet.)

In 2001, Google had 200 employees. In 2020 they had 135,301. That kind of meteoric growth could derail a company fast if they didn't focus. Google does. Google's mission is "To organize the world's information and make it universally accessible and useful."

On their company website's philosophy page, they are even more explicit. "It's best to do one thing really, really well. We do search."[55] Search is their niche.

Everything Google does supports their mission and their niche. Their Chrome browser enables a better online searching experience. Google Earth lets you search the world. They bought YouTube to help people share and access videos.

With tens of thousands of employees, Google generates lots of new products and services. In order to remain focused, Google regularly pares their offerings to the most successful and niche-related. They have eliminated 224 offerings to date (February 2021).[56] Some product eliminations, like the cessation of Google Reader, provoked outrage and protests among users. But the company's response was, "We need to focus."[57]

Google knows brands that focus flourish.

## The First Step is to Fight Fear

A niche is the remedy that brands suffering from FOMO and trying too hard to fit in need. Finding your niche requires that you first clear one major obstacle: fear.

The voices in your head can tell you there are no niches left in your industry to exploit. Or that you can kiss a chunk of your business goodbye the minute you commit to a niche. Or that the menial income you make from your least selling products is still profit in hand.

That's fear speaking. Don't listen.

Owners of brands in adolescence understandably hesitate to give up any hard-won business. That's not what I am telling you to do. What I am saying is that committing to a niche and guiding your brand toward it will result in a stronger brand in the long term, and more growth than you'd see by just winging it. Much more growth.

Niches take bravery and discipline. Your first brave act is to acknowledge the fear you have when it comes to narrowing your brand's scope. Allow yourself to detail the things you think will befall your brand if you do this. Write your feelings down or say them out loud. Naming fear disempowers it.

We're going to combat your fear with more than just will-power, don't worry. But you have to know the enemy before you can conquer it. Your enemy is not your competitors right now, it's your fear.

# Discovering Your Brand's Niche

Now that you've named your fears, let's get to the business of finding your brand's niche in a manner that conquers them with information and insights.

Begin by reviewing your sales reports. Answer these questions:

- Which products or services are truly driving the business?

- What are you doing that no one else is?

- Who are your best customers? Tap the Pareto principle, that 20 percent of your efforts result in 80 percent of your revenue. Identify the 20 percent.

Talk to your best customers to learn more about why they come to you. What are their biggest challenges? What situations prompt them to seek out your brand? What do they get from your brand that they don't get elsewhere? What do they enjoy about doing business with your brand?

Think about your brand purpose. Your niche will need to support it, and your purpose may well be the source of your niche when you think about it strategically.

Seek out a trusted advisor who knows your business well, but isn't as close to it as you are and can see it more objectively. Ask them what they think your brand's strengths are and what they know of your brand's reputation.

Identify potential niches among your brand strengths as evidenced in the concentration of your sales, your brand purpose, the uniqueness of what your brand offers, how your brand does business, and the reasons your best customers come to you. Look for common themes and threads through your business and all of your brand's constituencies.

For each potential niche, conduct a competitive analysis. Are you alone in the niche? If not, is it a crowded field? What is the market size? Do your research. The hope is to find an underserved market and become their go-to for the solution to their problem.

Confirm your chosen niche and allay your fear of focusing by verifying that the market size is ample enough for your brand to grow substantially. Remember, the market size just needs to be big enough for you to grow for several years. It does not need to be the biggest market in your field. In fact, some of the most successful niches come from the smaller markets that other brands ignore.

Niches not only help you grow your brand, but they make running the business easier because relevance to your niche becomes an easy litmus test for new product ideas, partnerships, marketing communications, and operational decisions.

## Be Open to Different Types of Niches

Remember this is a discovery process of a niche that is emerging from your brand in adolescence to help it focus and fight FOMO. When you discover the right niche, it may not be what you anticipated, but it should not be foreign to you. It's more of an aha moment than a complete surprise. It should feel plausible and right.

Niches can be:

Unique solutions to specific problems or conditions.

☐ Airbnb solves travelers' desire to feel like they belong in foreign locations.

☐ Spanx addresses "wardrobe woes," helping women look polished.

☐ Gluten Free Territory allows the gluten-allergic population to enjoy dessert without getting ill.

Well-defined target audiences, such as specific industries or groups of people.

☐ GemFind specializes in websites and digital strategy for jewelers.

☐ Under Armour serves the "scrappy outsider" athlete, the one who patiently looks on during the first few rounds of the draft pick and works to beat the odds.

☐ UPPAbaby caters to urban, fashion-conscious parents of young children with their stylish and highly functional strollers.

Attitudinal.

☐ Life is Good spreads optimism.

☐ Patagonia attracts people who have "a love of wild and beautiful places" and who want to "implement solutions to the environmental crisis."

- ☐ Crocs attracts people who want to be "comfortable in their own shoes."

Geographical.

- ☐ California Raisins benefit from the state's reputation as a sunny environment.

- ☐ Powell's City of Books prides themselves on being a Portland (Oregon) legend and the city's top attraction.

- ☐ Middlesex Savings Bank serves individuals and businesses in Middlesex County, Massachusetts, and has done so for 185 years.

Product-based, if the product is highly specialized.

- ☐ Swiss Army Knives remain the authentic multipurpose tool that many military personnel and campers seek.

- ☐ Rolex is synonymous with luxury watches.

- ☐ CB Stuffer built their reputation on peanut butter cups, and has the distinction of offering the largest one on the market.

Economic. (Though I am not a fan of this angle).

- ☐ Neiman Marcus appeals to high-end shoppers.

☐ Walmart is positioned as the retailer that helps you save money.

## Commit to Your Brand's Niche

Discovering your niche is the beginning of your work to counter FOMO. You need to implement your niche and remain true to it for your brand to become associated with it and then known for it. This is your second act of bravery, and is where the discipline comes in.

Once you have selected a niche, you and your team need to align your offerings, services, initiatives, and operations toward supporting that niche. What offerings fall outside your niche and should be cut from your product portfolio? Is your customer service designed to support your niche? What programs or initiatives support your niche and which ones should you discontinue?

After identifying and paring what does not fit your niche, assess where you can spend freed resources (inventory space, team time and effort, budget) to accelerate and solidify your leadership in your niche. What new training or information does your organization need to go full-throttle on your niche? What are the gaps in your product portfolio that you need to fill to serve your niche? What new product opportunities exist to fulfill related target market needs?

Perhaps the most difficult aspect of committing to your niche, you might find there are some customers you will no longer be able to serve, or should not serve as their requirements fall outside your niche. Identify them and then work with them to fulfill existing commitments and transition them to other providers, even if this means a competitor. Hey — I said this would take bravery and discipline, right? This is the true test of your commitment to your niche.

Learning to say no to customers who make requests well outside your brand's territory feels scary, but is empowering. It reinforces your brand's niche. If your brand is going to stand for something, it is going to have to say no to some things. But the depth of knowledge and expertise your brand team gains, the economies of scale you can achieve, and the clarity of focus are worth it.

## Focus Doesn't Just Help, It Can Be a Lifesaver

With The Chocolate Truffle and Bacci Chocolate Design on the brink of disaster in 2009, Erin Calvo-Bacci and her husband took a hard, in-depth look at their brands. What they saw was that the manufacturing side was carrying the business. All the retail costs were rising; packaging, heating, and staff most notably.

Erin's first step was to scale back the retail operations. She closed two of the three The Chocolate Truffle stores. Then she shifted the focus to their wholesale business, Bacci Chocolate Design.

Efforts to focus included moving the reliable staff Erin had hired for The Chocolate Truffle to the wholesale side. After Bacci Chocolate Design picked up key customers like The Paper Store and TJX in addition to numerous independents, Erin sold the remaining The Chocolate Truffle. Exiting brick-and-mortar retail, Bacci Chocolate Design rebranded as CB Stuffer and focused on selling their creations online.

"It was so much better working off a computer and not having the brick and mortar," said Erin.

Another aha moment helped Erin and Carlo focus the business further. "In 2010 we exhibited for the first time at the Fancy Food

Show. We brought everything but the kitchen sink — hand-dipped chocolates, peanut butter cups, etc. We saw that people really wanted the peanut butter cups." Erin knew they needed a way to stand out, and making the peanut butter cup their flagship product was the way.

Rather than hurt the business, Erin found life easier once she stopped Bacci Chocolate Design from trying to please everyone, and started focusing on their lead product. "For us, we had to do everything for everyone. Once we said we are going to focus on the peanut butter cup, it helped clear away a lot of clutter," she told me.[58]

Not only did the product provide their niche, but ultimately it became the company name.

Though Bacci Chocolate Design was named to reflect their ownership, the company suffered from confusion with Baci Perugina, an Italian purveyor of specialty chocolates. "They [prospects] would say they knew our product, they knew a chocolate called Bacci, but they didn't know us. Conversations would end because they thought they knew them."

Bacci Chocolate Design had named their peanut butter cup line CB Stuffer, so when they decided to have this line lead the brand, they renamed the brand CB Stuffer. This eliminated confusion and aligned their name with their niche.

Now instead of trying to please everyone, the CB Stuffer brand team concentrates on extending distribution to reach more fans which grows the business.

## Focusing on Being Yourself Works Best

Ultimately, the fake fronts Cady Heron put up and the exhaustion from toggling between the world of the Plastics, the wannabe-Aaron's-girlfriend world and the world of friends with Janis and Damian caught up with her.

Regina's fury over not being invited to Cady's party was eclipsed by her rage over Cady's deceptions, especially her ploy to trick her into eating weight-gain bars. Regina set out to frame Cady.

Aaron rejected Cady for becoming like Regina.

Janis and Damian became disgusted with her and renounced their friendship.

Turned away from the three worlds she had jostled to inhabit, Cady resigned herself to the rejection, and reverted to her kind and compassionate self, the way she was before trying to fit in.

After Cady confessed and owned her actions, things began to get better for her. She helped lead the Mathlete team to win a championship and was voted Spring Fling Queen.

Regina George joined the lacrosse team. "Finally girl world was at peace," Cady says at the end of the movie, but then Damian points out a set of three well-dressed freshmen strutting across campus and says, "Junior Plastics," indicating the next group to do battle with FOMO and the need to fit in.

# Key Takeaways from Suffering from FOMO and Trying Too Hard to Fit In

- Brands suffer from FOMO when they try to match their competitors' products and marketing from fear of losing sales for not having something their competitors do.

- The antidote to FOMO is for the brand to have a niche.

- Business owners shy away from niches for fear of lost business, but the idea that a niche hurts your business is a myth.

- Niches grow your business because they allow you to focus, develop in-depth knowledge of your target audience, guide decisions on new products and marketing, differentiate your brand and help make it your audience's go-to.

- Your biggest challenge to establishing a niche is your fear.

- Your best niche candidates come from the intersection of your brand strengths, your audience's needs, and a market big enough to support your growth for years. Establishing a niche that meets an unmet market need makes it easier to be the market leader.

- Niches can be attitudinal, geographical, unique solutions to problems, well-defined target audiences, product-based or economic.

# CHAPTER 7

# Needing to Make New Friends

## Signs Your Brand Needs New Friends

If you answer "Yes" to two or more of these questions, your brand may be in need of new friends/an additional target audience.

- Is finding new business among your target audience becoming increasingly difficult?

- Do your sales reports confirm your sales and customer numbers are relatively steady, but the number of new customers is few?

- Is your brand vulnerable to tremors or trauma in your primary market?

- Are your salespeople reporting lost opportunities because your brand lacks a companion product or area of service?

- Has a customer request led your brand to develop a new product or service that seems to fit naturally with your brand?

- Is there a pattern to requests that your brand turns down to stay true to its niche?

- Is there a market segment that has been clamoring for your brand, but that you have declined to serve to remain focused on your primary niche?

## When the Status Quo Doesn't Cut It Anymore

One afternoon in May 2007, I was volunteering at my daughter's elementary school after hours to help run a Brownie event for her girl scout troop. It focused on developing healthy exercise habits, and featured a number of physical challenges set up in the school auditorium. As the girls rotated through the stations, the soundtrack from *High School Musical* blared.

My daughter's friend's mother was working alongside me. When the song "Get Your Head in the Game" came on, she turned to me and confessed that she really loved this soundtrack. I smiled. I liked it too.

Though our daughters were only six at the time, *High School Musical* played regularly on the Disney Channel and was one of their favorites. Parents liked the catchy music, but also the adolescent themes we could relate to in the story.

While on a December break ski vacation, Troy Bolton (Zac Efron) and Gabriella Montez (Vanessa Hudgens) are cajoled by their respective parents to attend a ski lodge teen event. Despite not knowing each other and trying to lay low at the event, they are chosen to perform karaoke together. Hesitant at first, they are both surprised to discover their joy of singing as well as a mutual attraction.

Coincidentally, Gabriella, a high-achieving student who has led past academic teams to victory, has just transferred mid-year to East High School in Albuquerque, New Mexico, where Troy happens to be the star of the basketball team. They discover this coincidence in homeroom and share a long pause as they walk past the school musical audition sheet.

Both long to audition, but hesitate.

Troy worries about what his basketball teammate friends will think. Gabriella is grappling with trying to adjust and fit in at her new school. Classmate Sharpay, a domineering force in the drama club, discovers Gabriella's past and alerts Taylor, the Scholastic Decathalon team leader.

Troy and Gabriella fail to audition during the allotted time but Mrs. Darbus, the Drama Club director, overhears them singing and decides to give them a callback audition.

This news travels fast. Troy's friends are shocked that he and Gabriella have auditioned. Troy continues to ruminate over the potential consequences of pursuing something new that his current friends might not support.

Troy's gutsy move to audition inspires other students to confess their hidden hobbies, and the pressures they feel to "Stick to the Status Quo."

Troy's teammates Chad and Taylor conspire to pull the couple apart and derail their audition aspirations so they can protect their team's chances for victory. It appears Troy and Gabriella will have to choose between their known strengths and friends, and their new interest.

## Exploring New Interests via New Friend Groups

The onset of adolescence occurs during middle school, which includes grades six through eight in the United States and can start as early as fifth grade. Children who spent most of their days in a single classroom with a consistent set of classmates in elementary school now rotate to multiple classrooms with many new classmates.

The larger social population offers the opportunity for adolescents to change friend groups. Jaana Juvonen, a developmental psychologist at the University of California at Los Angeles, and her team recruited 6,000 sixth graders from 26 middle schools in 2010, and studied their friendship habits over the course of three years. They found that two-thirds of children entering middle school changed friends between the fall and the spring of that year.[59]

Adolescence also brings a neural remodeling of the brain to prepare it for adulthood. Neurological changes encourage adolescents to try new things and experiences.[60]

When middle schoolers change friends, they gravitate toward those who share their interests or a new interest they are exploring — theater, tennis, soccer, robotics. This continues during high school, college and even later — the adolescent brain does not reach its fully maturity until the mid-20s.

New friend groups support adolescents' exploration into new interests and foster their growth by allowing them to break free of pre-existing social orders that may have felt constricting. This is similar to Troy being known as the basketball star, and having his teammates dissuade him from pursuing theater believing it might take his head out of the game.

Making new friends does not necessarily mean ditching old

ones. But it might mean shifting focus to the new group when the old one is no longer supporting you.

## A Bright Light Suddenly Goes Dark

In 2008, Lucy Dearborn had a thriving lighting store business called Lucía Lighting & Design in Lynn, Massachusetts. Lucía Lighting & Design specialized in medium- to high-end lighting fixtures and served the North Shore, which is the coastal region of Massachusetts from north of Boston to the New Hampshire border.

In 2005, she and a partner transformed a funeral home mansion into a first-class lighting showroom. Using her contacts and her 10+ years of lighting business experience, Lucía Lighting & Design logged $1 million in revenue their first year. Lucy deepened her relationships with contractors and interior designers on the North Shore. Three years in, they had as much business as they could handle.

Then the Great Recession hit. New construction on the North Shore stopped cold. The abrupt and sharp decline shocked Lucy. She found herself scrounging for business where it had been so easy just months before.

# New Markets and Niches as New Friend Groups

It is natural for brands to reach a point where they have acquired as much market share as they are going to get. The brand's growth levels off because that segment has taken them as far as it can. In order to grow, the brand needs a new market segment, a "new friend group" to expand its circle.

This is akin to teenagers who find they have new interests

beyond those of their existing friend group. They don't abandon these friends, but to continue their personal growth they seek out new friend groups who share those new interests.

Sometimes business owners find this situation thrust upon them like Lucy did. Other times, the plateau happens naturally. In those cases, it is up to the business owner and brand team to realize the situation and to begin qualifying a new market segment.

New market segments that are specialties also qualify as new niches. As we saw in Chapter 6, niches help build a name for your brand and make it the go-to for that target audience. Assembling numerous niches that jive with your purpose is a powerful way to grow a brand.

## Add Niches to Grow

Jay Myers built his company by starting with one niche and adding new ones as opportunity and capacity allowed.

In 1995, Jay had the unenviable experience of being laid off on his 39th birthday. He had built a profitable $5 million video conference division for his employer from scratch. Jay learned early on that he was "not suited for the corporate world."[61] His firing was the last time he was going to allow his destiny to be decided by "suits" who did not share his interests and who were willing to sacrifice his profitable division because the parent company had financial troubles.

Jay decided to leverage his knowledge of the young video conference industry and start his own company. "Video conferencing was and is a fairly small niche. We started with a stupid simple strategy: concentrate on something bigger company competitors weren't."[62]

Within video conferencing, Jay and his initial team focused even further on corporate clients. Jay's former employer targeted higher education customers for their video conference business. Jay knew the corporate market would yield better profit margins.

But while Jay and his initial team focused on one niche, they had their eye on eventually serving more audiences.

"We actually struggled to nail down a name and logo for the company at first: we tossed out quite a few names like Video Visions and Video Innovations before deciding on Interactive Solutions Incorporated (ISI), partly because it did not tie us down to selling only video products. We wanted to be a provider of technology and engineering solutions that had a particular expertise in video conferencing."[63]

ISI's second niche arrived organically in 1998. ISI received a request to install a telemedicine conferencing system. It was a challenge, but in meeting it ISI's team learned much about telemedicine video conferencing installations and saw the potential in the healthcare marketplace.

ISI stalled just before the Great Recession from 2005-2007 at annual revenue of about $11-12 million each year.[64] The brand was 9-11 years old during this time.

At this point, Jay's experience with higher education came in handy. ISI pitched in-state colleges and universities to handle their long-distance learning and audio-visual technology needs. Higher education became ISI's third niche and got sales growth rolling again.

"It's interesting to see how many entrepreneurs tend to 'plateau' their businesses and careers because they lose their appetite for risk," Jay writes in his book *Hitting the Curveballs*.[65] By their willingness to take calculated risks and expand into new niches, "ISI has evolved from a single-track start-up struggling to survive to a multimillion-dollar-a-year company with installations in 40 US states and 15 international sites."[66]

Of brand adolescence Jay said, "I absolutely believe that's what happened to us. We had to rebuild the business over and over and reinvent ourselves."

Jay was not only savvy about the management of risk, but he also had great self-awareness for his own risk tolerance. When Jay and I spoke in May 2018, he told me he knew ISI, which took in $17 million in revenues in 2017, could be a $40-50 million company. To get there though, he would need to acquire a company. "But I'll be 62 in December. I don't have tolerance for that kind of risk."

On October 31, 2018, Jay sold ISI to AVI-SPL, an industry leader in the audio-visual solutions world, after securing a leadership role for his son, benefits and career opportunities for his employee team, and confidence that AVI-SPL would take excellent care of ISI's customers.

Jay switched to a business development manager role when the acquisition was announced and stayed through December 2019.

## Dangers of Needing to Make New Friends: Sudden Loss of Revenue, Rising Customer Acquisition Costs, Missed Upsell Opportunities

While a primary niche helps a brand stand for something, gain traction based on that stand, and grow, reliance on a single niche does present some risk. As we saw with Lucía Lighting & Design, if the niche experiences a sharp downturn or other trauma, it can take your brand's revenue down with it.

If you've maxed out your initial niche — gotten as much business or as many customers as your brand can — you may find that luring new customers takes more time, more employee effort, and more marketing dollars than it used to. Rising customer acquisition costs can squeeze your margins and require longer customer engagements or larger orders to recoup them. Ultimately it can become prohibitively expensive to continue to hunt for customers in that niche.

Your brand may also be turning away potential customers who are naturally attracted to your brand because their problems align with the problem it solves. Prospects who approach you often have knowledge and some level of trust in your brand already, making them stronger sales leads. The cost of acquiring these customers is often less than that those you court cold. Not serving these customers can mean higher customer acquisition costs than necessary too.

When your brand needs new friends, it may be failing to address customer problems that are related to your area of expertise, but not squarely in your niche. Existing customers who can't get all of those related issues solved with your brand are forced to look at competitors for the areas your brand does not serve, opening you up to unnecessary competition and forgoing an upsell opportunity. Upselling current customers is a strong source of brand growth, as the customer acquisition cost is very low or zero and the margin is thus higher than courting a new customer.

## Lucía Lighting's Plan B

Seeing that the North Shore construction business had come to a halt, Lucy noticed the only real construction was happening in Boston. She began aggressively courting the Boston market.

The Boston design community held networking events every Tuesday. So, each Tuesday Lucy laced up her sneakers and walked around new construction sites in Boston to introduce herself and Lucía Lighting, to hand out business cards, and to attend the networking events.

"We were a solid Plan A for the North Shore — the customer relationships were there already. My goal was to become a solid Plan B for Boston designers and builders. They were losing their lighting account reps. I told them that my staff were seasoned experts and that they would get to talk to the same people each time, getting their expertise. And if you want to talk to the business owner you are doing so now and can contact me."[67]

Lucy's Tuesday pound-the-pavement strategy slowly got the Boston construction market aware of Lucía Lighting & Design and saved the business. She worked every day with her staff to gain trust among her new customers and maintain trust among her existing customers from the North Shore. The Recession resulted in a five-year stall of the business, but it did not die.

Finally, business began growing again in 2014. Lucía Lighting did $3 million in 2018 and had 12 employees, some full-time and some part-time.[68]

The Great Recession forced an early brand adolescence on Lucía Lighting & Design. Lucy recognized the answer as adding a new target audience to her brand. Her new geographical market segment not only saved the business, but it also expanded the company's reach, providing growth when the economy came back.

## Plan Growth with Proactive Niche Assessment

Brands that need new friends — because they have maxed out

their niche or because their niche has suffered a trauma — solve their problem by identifying an additional niche.

If you find your brand needing new friends, remember not to give up on the primary audience that is still fueling your business. Make sure those customers continue to receive excellent service. Then turn your attention to qualifying a new friend group — either a new audience or a new niche.

Lucy's quick thinking and hard work saved Lucía Lighting & Design by adding a new geographical niche to the brand. If you can foresee the need for a new niche and proactively choose one, you may fare better than if your brand is under duress.

To qualify a new audience or a new niche for your brand, look for an audience that relates to your brand purpose and has needs aligned with what your brand does well. The good news is that you may have a running start.

## Generating Niche Ideas

Your running start is an existing organic lead you may have, like Jay Myers at ISI did after a client asked his video conferencing company to install a telemedicine video conferencing system. He realized ISI could leverage that knowledge in an area where there was likely more demand for telemedicine. Or like we saw in Chapter 4, when Spenser Brosseau's photo booth business attracted wedding clients to Spike Entertainment.

Keeping your eyes open for possible future niches can save you time when you need to consider niche ideas. This is why mining organic requests is the first step to generating niche ideas.

1. **Mine Organic Requests.** Customer requests are evidence that a fruitful market may exist. Your first step to selecting

a new niche is to review requests your company has gotten
and see if there are leads there to a new niche.

Have any of your employees suggested a new niche or
market segment for your brand based on their contact with
customers? Employees are an often-underutilized source of
niche and market ideas. Lucy Dearborn of Lucía Lighting &
Design realized this as she was working through her brand's
adolescence. She told me, "Putting faith in people's skill sets
and letting them help grow the business. Good ideas — doesn't
matter where they come from."

2. **Review and Research Your Existing Customer Base.**
   Mine your customer service and sales reports. Do research
   to better understand who is buying your products, and see
   if there is a secondary audience already showing promise
   that you had not noticed before. Deliberately targeting an
   audience where some customers have already found their
   way to your brand can be an easy and less risky way to
   grow the business.

   Jay Myers at ISI does this often. His advice to me: "[You've]
   got to continuously look at elements that continue to grow
   the business and balance that with a tolerance for risk. You
   can invest a ton of money in something dicey or look at a
   low-level entry point that is complementary [to your current
   business]."

3. **Conduct an Industry Review.** Your third step is to take
   time to look at your industry and see where the action is.
   While you don't want to follow any trend randomly, new
   market needs that crop up related to your brand strengths
   can be a good source of new niches. While the Great

Recession compelled Lucy Dearborn to take a strategic look at her industry and find a new audience for Lucía Lighting & Design, looking at your industry periodically without that pressure is a healthier way to grow your brand. It is also a helpful way to stay current on trends and developments.

When I interviewed Jay Myers at ISI initially, he told me, "[We are] exploring selling security systems. [Our techs] are walking in and people are doing that while they install the audiovisual. We are also getting knowledgeable to support cybersecurity."

4. **Brainstorm.** Armed with your organic requests, customer research, and industry review, brainstorm ideas for new niche opportunities. Can you sell your existing offerings to a similar audience in a new geographical region like Lucy Dearborn did? Can you parlay your current expertise into an offering for a market segment already on your radar like Jay Myers did? Are there other areas your team feels it is worth to explore?

5. **Consult a trusted advisor.** Board members and other trusted advisors who are familiar with your market but less immersed may be a good source of potential niche ideas. They may also be able to provide insights on ideas you and your team have generated and to help you make connections in the new market.

# Vetting Your Niche Ideas

Once you have one or several potential niche ideas, vet them the way you would any audience or niche.

1. **Determine the market size.** Is it big enough? You need plenty of running room for your brand. Is the market trending up or down? You want a growing market or one that is at least stable.

2. **Can your brand own the niche?** Would your brand be alone in the niche? If not, how crowded is the field? Do you have an opportunity to claim this niche or is it already associated with another brand? Customer research can help here, and it can be as simple as asking, "When you think of [insert niche], what comes to mind?" Aim for niches you can own or be a major player in. Owning is best.

3. **Understand the circumstances** that prompt the audience in this niche to seek out your product or service and where they get their information when they are looking to buy. Will your existing expertise apply or give you a running start in this niche? Second niches come more easily when your expertise helps your organization get up to speed faster and brings credibility that helps your new audience trust your brand with the niche.

4. **Assess the feasibility and logistics** of serving the niche to ensure you can do so efficiently and in a cost-effective manner. Is your organization equipped to serve the niche?

Do you need new equipment, partners, distributors? Will the logistics be easy and smooth or challenging and risky?

5. **Take inventory of existing relationships that can help you.** If you need partners, distributors or other resources to reach the new niche, are any of your existing ones positioned to support your brand? Who can help your brand get introduced and established with the new audience?

6. **Evaluate the potential for repeat business** and beneficial long-term relationships. Choose a niche that will generate long-term customers over transient ones. Repeat business helps keep your customer acquisition costs down and your profit margin up. Plus, good long-term customer relationships add joy to your business and are an asset to your brand.

## Prepare Before You Launch

You get one shot at making a great first impression. You want your brand's new friends to have that great first impression.

Once you have qualified a new target market or niche, prepare for the launch internally first. Make sure your organization is equipped to handle the expansion so you can deliver the best possible customer experience to your new audience.

In Jay Myers' book, *Hitting the Curveballs,* he wrote about navigating the ups and downs of ISI's growth. He advised three things to support growth:[69]

1. Have enough staff to handle the new volume of sales and

customer support. Make sure your staff are qualified to engage with this new market.

2. Maintain tight controls on accounts receivable to meet cash flow obligations. Growth often requires investment in additional staff, product, and resources. You want to ensure you can cover your obligations while funding growth.

3. Have access to capital or a line of credit to provide you with a cash flow back-up as you grow.

To Jay's three pieces of advice, I add a fourth:

4. Ensure you have the inventory or offering ready. A premature launch can squash a new market trajectory before it achieves any traction. Your initial impressions are crucial to generating positive word-of-mouth to your new target. To the best extent possible, test your new product to increase the likelihood of wowing your customers and nix any true barriers to embracing it. Road test new processes and services to make sure the first customer-facing deliveries are successful.

## Find Your Kelsi

So how does *High School Musical* play out?

After Mrs. Darbus, the Drama Club director of East High School, informs Troy and Gabriella that they failed to audition during the allotted time, Kelsi, the quiet composer of the musical and piano accompanist, gets up to leave the piano and drops her sheet music. Troy and Gabriella help her pick up the pages. Kelsi plays the audition tune for them as it is supposed to sound, and Troy and Gabriella sing.

Mrs. Darbus overhears them and grants them a callback. She tells Kelsi to work with them to prepare.

As a new friend with no preconceived notions about Troy and Gabriella, Kelsi has no trouble seeing the two of them as talented singers. She energetically supports their development as singers and clears obstacles to their success.

While Troy and Gabriella grapple with the basketball and Scholastic Decathalon team reactions to their callbacks, Kelsi helps them rehearse. When Sharpay gets the callbacks switched to a time that conflicts with the basketball championship and the academic decathalon, Kelsi gets wind of it and helps organize the now-supportive friends on both teams to help Troy and Gabriella's callback happen.

This is Disney, so of course Troy and Gabriella pull off a rousing callback and win the lead parts in the musical.

If your brand is in need of new friends, find the new niche that is your Kelsi to get back to growth mode.

# Key Takeaways from Needing to Make New Friends

- Brands needing to make new friends bump up against the limit of business they can get from their primary niche or suffer a decline when that niche is compromised due to recession or other trauma.

- These brands solve their problem by identifying and entering one or more additional niches.

- Brands that strategically keep an eye out for their next niche once their primary one is established have an easier time than those who seek secondary niches under duress.

- The best and most successful subsequent niches have a head start from the brand's existing relationships, products, and expertise.

# CHAPTER 8

# Defending Your Varsity Team Spot

## Signs Your Brand Needs to Defend Its Varsity Team Spot

If your response is "Yes" to two or more of these questions, your brand may need to defend its varsity team position in your niche.

- Is it harder to find new customers than it used to be?

- Does gaining a new customer mean you must steal them away from a competitor?

- Are your customers reevaluating your relationship or existing contracts based on overtures from your competitors?

- Are your customers challenging your prices based on bids from your competitors more than in the past?

- Are your vendors and sources having trouble meeting your demand because they are also supplying your competitors?

- Do prospects or customers ask if you will match a competitor's new approach or offering?

- Has a longtime customer suddenly asked you to start providing bids when your prices were not challenged before?

## When Your Past Performance No Longer Makes the Cut

On May 24, 1984, a future basketball star was born in Brooklyn, NY. Several years later, he moved south of the Mason-Dixon line with his mother, who pushed him to stay on top of his schoolwork.

He began playing basketball at a young age and fell in love with the game. His mother used his love of the game to keep him in line by threatening to deny access to any basketball court for even a minor transgression. Springtime was especially sweet. He reveled in the NCAA March Madness tournament followed by the NBA playoffs.[70]

He would later help his college win the NCAA tournament in his freshman year.

Upon arriving at high school, he tried out for the varsity basketball team. Despite his love of the game and hard work, he failed to make the cut.

That failure was a wake-up call. Being knowledgeable, immersed, and practiced was not enough to rise to the top of the roster. What did it take to turn this player into a basketball star?

# The Level of Competition Rises in Adolescence

When adolescent athletes transition from middle school to high school, they often face a narrowing of opportunities to play their preferred sport. Travel teams and recreational leagues that existed during their elementary and middle school years don't often exist at the high school level. As a result, teens often find the high school team is their sole opportunity to continue to play.

High schools often bring together teens from multiple middle schools. This means the number of competitors may rise at the same time that the number of team slots shrinks.

More players vying for fewer spots makes for more intense competition, especially for those who aim to play at the varsity level.

High school students who make the cut for the varsity team tend to share common traits that set them apart from their competitors. Confidence. A deep capacity to focus. Exceptional preparation that gives them superior techniques and tactics, increases their stamina, and makes them physically fit. A joy for playing that helps them relax in crucial moments and come through in the clutch. And often a physique that gives them a size or speed advantage.

Brands that stand out in their industry exhibit similar advantages.

## Finding Space in an Open Playing Field

After her divorce in the late 1990s, Stephanie Blackwell was seeking to leave the alfalfa sprout business she co-owned with her ex-husband and start a company of her own. When a gourmet retailer who she was pitching for the old business asked her to package their private-label snacks instead, Stephanie recognized an opportunity and seized it.

Stephanie's business acumen led her to study the opportunity more broadly. She found little competition existed in the business of packing snacks. This was the entrepreneurial opportunity she'd been looking for.

With that initial account, she launched her business by packing whatever snacks customers requested. She leased 1,000 square feet and hired four employees, financing the company initially with her credit cards. Her first-year revenue was $900,000.

"I was mopping floors, sweeping, packing. Working 65-75 hours a week. I didn't know what a weekend was. I was having a blast owning my own business."[71]

Within a year, the business moved to a 7,000-square-foot space. For the first four years, the business packed private-label product for other companies.

In the fifth year, Stephanie started her own brand, Aurora Products, and began offering Aurora-branded snacks. Her branded products helped her land supermarket chain Ahold as a customer. Others followed, along with national warehouse clubs like BJ's and Costco, and specialty retailers like TJ Maxx, Marshall's, and Christmas Tree Shops.

Stephanie aimed for steady growth. She did not want to borrow money, and she ploughed earnings back into the business to fund growth.

Several years into the business, Stephanie's entrepreneurial radar pointed toward an opportunity to work with Whole Foods.

"At first we packed what they [my customers] wanted me to. As the business got older, we got involved with Whole Foods which has definite guidelines of what they would accept. We started following those guide rules. I liked them."

Whole Foods' guidelines required all-natural fruit, nuts, and candies in their snacks. Packing both "regular" dried fruit, nuts, and candies alongside all-natural ones posed a logistical challenge and risked mix-ups. Stephanie decided to eliminate those risks by committing to all-natural and organic snacks only. Her customers liked that dedication. Aurora Products became known for it.

Declaring Aurora Products' all-natural niche meant losing customers who wanted items like trail mixes with M&Ms or gummy bears or who did not want to pay extra for pure vanilla or chocolate. But the niche decision strengthened the brand. Stephanie felt supporting the Aurora Natural product line this way was worthwhile. The line expanded to include salad toppings and granolas.

By 2011, Aurora Products operated in a 75,000-square-foot facility, the employee count had risen to more than 150, and sales registered close to $40 million. The company later moved to a 140,000-square-foot facility in Orange, Connecticut and added another 50 employees.

As consumer health trends accelerated, more and more competitors entered the all-natural snack manufacturing realm. Where there had been white space and an unmet market need, the all-natural snack packing industry soon became popular and crowded.

At 18 years old, Aurora Products hit their brand adolescence. Sales plateaued. It became very difficult to get a new account. Stephanie told me, "The last three years the growth has leveled off. There's so much competition out there. When we first got involved there was no one in the market. Now there are people my size that are being bought out."

# Opportunity Attracts Competition

Entrepreneurs who identify unmet market needs and fill them often have the luxury of being alone in the market for a while. Would-be competitors either have not yet discovered the need or will wait to see if the niche pioneers prosper. Being first to meet those needs often means owning that niche.

Owning a niche lets the first brand that corners the market develop a commanding lead and deep expertise. Concerted efforts to expand brands' territories and customer base help them get out of start-up mode and establish themselves in the niche before the rest of the world realizes how lucrative their space is.

But eventually the world wakes.

Profitable niches attract competitors, particularly those in markets on an upward trend. Niches that may have initially appeared to be peripheral and small become more mainstream and magnets for both entrepreneurs and major industry players.

Brands in adolescence that got their start by discovering and exploiting white space can feel like they are suddenly trying to hold their spot in the market if hordes of competitors enter. Economic opportunists abound. Business owners and investors are more likely to pursue a new venture in a proven niche than initiate their own. When competitors flood in, the space is no longer white.

When Federal Express had sufficiently convinced the world that overnight shipping was not only feasible but preferable to the US Post Office (USPS), numerous companies joined the industry. Once Airbnb proved that renting someone's home for a vacation was not creepy but cozier than a hotel, other short-stay home rental services popped up. Spotify's success at attracting subscribers to stream music legally has now got Apple and Amazon chasing it.

Niche pioneers do the hard work of educating the world on the value of their niche, and get rewarded with followers crashing their party. Such is the advantage of being first.

But the value of being first does not disappear with the party crashers. Done right, you can remind the world that you were first and that your brand remains the go-to for your niche. Let's look at how Federal Express, Airbnb, and Spotify coped with challenges to their niches.

## Federal Express Becomes FedEx Overnight

Do you remember when FedEx was Federal Express?

When Federal Express launched in the United States in 1973, nationwide overnight delivery seemed like a pipe dream. The concept was so far-fetched that Xerox shipped empty boxes for two weeks before entrusting them with document-filled ones.

The initial job of the Federal Express brand was to represent speed and reliability. Hence the tagline, "When it absolutely, positively has to be there overnight." Creative approaches to emphasizing their speed resulted in entertaining commercials starring fast talker John Moschitta.

By the early 1990s, with their reliability and speed established, Federal Express was going global.

While the word "federal" had given the company credibility in the US as an alternative to the post office in 1973, it was now conjuring images of the federales in Latin America. (Federales are the Mexican federal police and also a faction that fought in the Argentine Civil War in the 1800s.) It was also hard for people in other parts of the world to pronounce.

Meanwhile, competitor Emery had copied Federal Express' model by getting their own planes. Airborne Express entered the small package air express business. The USPS began pushing their own overnight delivery service. United Parcel Service (UPS), the largest shipper via trucks, entered the air shipping business and DHL Worldwide Courier Express Network replicated Federal Express' US model overseas.

Customers now had more choices. Federal Express saw the need to reassert their market leadership.

To the eyes of the world they did it overnight, on June 24, 1994. I remember because my husband and I were on our honeymoon in Greece during that time. When we returned to the US, Federal Express as we knew them were gone.

Every company truck, plane, package, and envelope from the former Federal Express now said FedEx. It was weird, but easy to understand. The verb "to fedex" had been in our business lexicon for a few years by then. It was shorter and easier to pronounce.

Executing the transformation overnight emphasized the company's speed and superior logistical skills. It also won them extensive press coverage equivalent to millions of dollars in advertising.

The company's overnight transformation turned out to be the culmination of two years of research and rebranding work. The impetus for the work was that the company's audience and offerings had grown. The company needed to evolve their brand to encompass the breadth of what they did and to be relevant to new audiences. But it also had to fend off the competitors challenging their space.

## Airbnb Defines Their Brand Identity to Reassert Market Leadership

Airbnb went from a homestay service in 2008 that few would trust to a business booking 6 million stays and earning $250 million in revenue in 2013, and scoring a $10 billion valuation in early 2014. While several competitors were founded prior to Airbnb (Vacation-Rental-By-Owner VRBO in 1995, HomeAway in 2004, Booking.com in 1996, FlipKey in 2006), it was Airbnb's success that confirmed the viability of the homestay concept and fueled industry growth. And it was this success that attracted many market entrants including Roomkey, ThirdHome, Homestay, TurnKey, and Outdoorsy.

As Airbnb took off, founder Brian Chesky realized the company needed help defining the Airbnb brand. He approached brand expert Douglas Atkin in late 2012 for help. Atkin's response was that the company first needed to find its purpose.

Atkin and a small group of Airbnb employees conducted inter-views with 485 Airbnb community members — hosts, guests, and employees — all over the world. The research yielded the insight that people yearned to belong wherever they went. The success of the research also led Chesky to offer Atkin a job as global head of community. From this insight also came the purpose of the company: "Creating a world where Anyone can Belong Anywhere."

A purpose that comes from the community resonates with the community. Airbnb then refocused and restructured them-selves around this purpose. This took time. By the time Chesky introduced the Airbnb rebrand in July 2014, all aspects of the company's operations and communications had been revised with the "belong anywhere" purpose in mind.

By defining Airbnb's purpose and announcing it publicly, Airbnb committed to shifting from a homestay provider to a purpose-driven brand. And they began the work of separating themselves from their homestay competitors with the distinction of being the brand that helped people "Belong Anywhere." By laying claim to an identity that is a driver of other homestay companies, Airbnb reasserted their market and niche leadership.

## Spotify Innovates and Evolves Identity to Stay Ahead of the Pack

When I first heard the name Spotify, it conjured an image of a laundry pre-wash treatment product like Tide's stain removal sticks. Little did I know.

Spotify is a music streaming service founded in Sweden in 2006 and launched in 2008. Co-founder and current CEO Daniel Ek had a lifelong passion for music and wanted to provide a way for listeners to legally stream the songs they wanted to listen to. Services including Pandora (November 2000), Slacker Radio (March 2007), Deezer (August 2007), and iHeartRadio (April 2008) all launched with the same goal. Most of these services offered radio-like streaming experiences.

By contrast, Spotify gave users control, letting them select specific songs, create their own playlists, and collaborate on playlists. Spotify also focused on growing their music catalog quickly to rival iTunes. This approach helped Spotify gain more traction than their competitors.

After a few years, Spotify's success began to gain attention in the industry. Google, Apple, and Amazon all entered the fray between 2011 and 2016. After enjoying a sizable market lead over early rivals, Spotify realized their new deep-pocketed tech competitors had name recognition, large audiences, and other revenue streams to fund their market entry. They would ramp up fast to invade Spotify's space.

Spotify's management responded by conducting a company-wide redefinition of the brand's values, accelerating their subscription efforts, exploiting their playlist abilities, and leveraging their vast data stores. The brand also redefined their mission. In short, Spotify launched a full-court press to run further and faster than its rivals.

Spotify calls employees "band members" and considers their culture a brand strength. In 2014, Spotify's HR department embarked on an effort to redefine the company's core values so that they resonated with everyone in the band. Dubbed "The Passion Tour," extensive workshops and voting resulted in five core values: innovative, collaborative, sincere, passionate, and playful, each with brief elaborations.[72]

While rallying the band at home, Spotify management raced to grab more market share by introducing family subscriptions ($14.99 per month for up to six family members) and student plans ($4.99 per month) in 2014. In 2017, Spotify upped the ante by adding Hulu access to the student plan, and in 2018 they added Showtime.

The family and student plans supercharged subscription growth. Spotify ended 2013 with 6 million paid subscribers and 24 million active users. Those figures soared to 108 million subscribers and 232 million monthly active users as of the second quarter of 2019.[73]

Spotify added new curated playlists and features to their collaborative playlists that allowed users to see who contributed and when. Users loved these features. My daughter mentioned that her tennis team collaborated on a playlist to psych themselves up for matches.

Spotify's early lead in active users also provided a trove of data that they began to leverage in their relationship with artists in 2015 with the launch of Fan Insights. Fan Insights helped artists understand the profile and location of their listeners so they could market their music and site concerts more effectively.

In October 2017, Spotify relaunched Fan Insights as Spotify for Artists, providing acts with a profile page and more tools to manage their business.

Spotify's original mission was "Give people access to all the music they want all the time — in a completely legal and accessible way," but clearly several companies were chasing this goal now. As brand visionary, CEO Ek introduced a new mission in his Founder's letter when Spotify filed for their IPO in February 2018, "To unlock the potential of human creativity — by giving a million creative artists the opportunity to live off their art and billions of fans the opportunity to enjoy and be inspired by it."

With 155 million subscribers as of the end of 2020,[74] Spotify is the music-streaming industry leader. Apple Music is second with 60 million[75] and Amazon is third with 55 million.[76] Google is struggling to manage and merged Google Play Music and YouTube Music, with a total of 15 million users.[77] So far Spotify's full-court press is paying off.

# Dangers of Failing to Defend Your Varsity Team Spot: Diminished Differentiation, Lost Customers, Business Decline

If your competition invades your brand's market position so much that your brand no longer stands out, it's like getting demoted to junior varsity or even an intramural team. Your brand gets relegated to the pack of second-tier choices.

Being second tier makes it much harder to attract customers or retain the ones you have. Prospects who may have considered you in the past may not even find or include your brand in their consideration set. Competitors who show greater target audience knowledge, provide better services or offer superior products may appeal more to prospects and lure your current customers away.

Declining new customer counts and a shrinking customer base will decrease your revenues. Your brand may have to fight harder to acquire new customers, pushing up marketing costs and narrowing your profit margins. Falling revenues also tend to put your brand in defense mode, taking your attention and resources away from long-term, brand-enhancing activities and shifting it to short-term survival tactics.

When your varsity team spot is challenged, ruing the crowd or going somewhere else are not your best options. Deepening your commitment and finding a way to reassert your niche leadership are.

# Upping Your Brand's Game

Let's take a minute upfront to talk about how you should NOT react to having your niche invaded.

## Don't Cut Your Prices

Regardless of your niche, do not respond by lowering your prices.

Resist the urge to beat your competitors on price to steal market share or lure new customers. This literally and figuratively cheapens your brand. It adds no value, only subtracts. And it is a short-term fix, especially if you are erasing margins you don't have to spare.

Price competition is a punt, and tells outsiders that your brand has not mustered its differentiation and has not built its value sufficiently to justify the price you ask. If that is the case, bolster your differentiation, your niche, and the value you offer instead.

There is also no next step after cutting your price, except cutting your price more. This begins a downward spiral that is hard to escape. The only way back up is to increase value.

Now that we have sidestepped that land mine, let's get to approaches that will help.

If your brand needs to defend its varsity spot, the best way is to reassert your brand leadership in your niche. It's the classic best-defense-is-a-great-offense approach. And like Fedex, Airbnb, and Spotify, it means going deeper into your niche, not running away.

1. **Clarify your brand identity and evolve it if needed.** I am not talking about a superficial logo update here. I am talking about strategic evaluations to ensure your purpose and attributes are still relevant and reflect your brand, and that your stated and practiced values are the same. If your brand began in an open white space and now competes intensely for that same terrain, your market is likely to have changed. Your brand may need to evolve to continue to serve your market well and to retain your niche leadership.

   You'll want to conduct a competitive analysis. See Chapter 9 for help with that. You are looking to understand your competitors' identities and market position so that you can clarify your brand's identity and market position and communicate it well.

   Talk to your customers, employees, and other constituents about their views of your brand and its role in the marketplace. Is it still your customers' go-to? Do employees feel the brand is living its values? Or if you have not yet codified those, now is the time (see Chapter 5). Do employees feel the brand is well positioned to lead the market? Are there opportunities they see that you need to consider?

   Think of this step as shoring up your home base. You want your employees, customers, and other constituents to be happy with your brand and prefer it over your competition. You need to be clear about your brand's identity and values so they can be too, and so they can feel good about supporting them.

   If you make changes, take the time to operationalize them so they permeate the organization. Communicate them internally and externally.

In some cases, a brand evolution may involve tweaks in the way you serve customers, in your offerings, in your operations, and — yes — in your logo and communications. This is less evolution than a brand "refresh," but serves to keep your brand current.

In other cases, a brand evolution can involve major changes and quantum leaps to catch up with the role your brand plays in your audience's lives and your marketplace — just like Airbnb's discovery of their purpose. And like FedEx's name change, which acknowledged their leadership position and rewarded their audience by taking their new name from their vernacular.

These bolder changes were reflected in new logos and visual representations, but those were an outcome of the strategic work that powered the brand's evolution, not just a creative update. That said, a logo refresh or redesign done well can garner the attention your brand needs to communicate your changes and your sharpened brand identity.

2. **Deepen your brand's relationship with your audience by doubling down on your niche.** One benefit of being first to market is that many customers and market stakeholders knew your brand before your competitors. After clarifying your brand, capitalize on your lead and established relationships by deepening them. The research you do for your brand clarification can also serve this strategy by updating you on what matters to your audience, what their concerns are, what needs remain unmet.

Conduct research among the core customers in your niche to understand how well your brand and your products are serving them. Make improvements where needed. Listen for new and additional opportunities to help customers solve the problem your brand addresses.

Leverage your knowledge and relationships with your audience by wowing them in new ways. Demonstrate your commitment to them by fulfilling unmet needs and providing new offerings and opportunities.

The specific way your brand doubles down may depend on the type of niche you have. Here are some examples of what your brand could do based on the six types of niches I introduced in Chapter 6:

    a.  Unique solutions to specific problems or conditions

    b.  Well-defined target audiences such as specific industries or groups of people

    c.  Attitudinal

    d.  Geographical

    e.  Product-based (for specialized products)

    f.  Economic

1. **Unique solutions to specific problems or conditions.** What issues you might not have addressed arise in solving the problem or condition? What conditions precede or follow use of your offering that you could address to improve your customers' experience and grow your brand? How can your brand deepen its relationship with customers by addressing an adjacent issue?

   When FedEx pulled off their overnight brand transformation on June 24, 1994, they reminded customers and the public that they personified speed and reliability. But FedEx did not stop there.

   Shortly afterward, they began investing in tracking software and systems so customers could not only have faith that the brand would deliver on time, they could get proof of where their package was in the process. FedEx no doubt heard that even with their brand promise, customers were anxious about packages arriving on time while they were in transit. FedEx looked for ways to deepen their relationship with customers by allaying their anxiety.

In the process of addressing this customer need, FedEx built a proprietary tracking system that further differentiated their commitment to reliable and speedy delivery. The tracking option proved highly desirable among customers. Rivals were forced to follow to compete.

FedEx also created the first automated package shipping system for PCs and, in the mid-1990s, was one of the first companies to enable business-to-business transactions on its website.[78] Noting their customers' international business dealings, FedEx expanded overseas, becoming authorized to serve China in 1995. Through an acquisition from Evergreen International Airlines, they became the sole US cargo-only carrier with aviation rights to China.

In February 2004, FedEx bought privately-held Kinko's and branded them FedEx Kinko's (and, in 2008, FedEx Office), giving the brand 1,200 outposts to expand their reach to customers and make it more convenient.[79]

FedEx maintains their lead in the overnight shipping industry by constantly looking for ways to enhance their customers' experience.

2. **Well-defined target audiences such as specific industries or groups of people.** If your niche is a very specific audience, look for ways to reinforce your value to them and to serve them more. Like Pat Flynn did.

Pat Flynn started a website to help himself study for an architecture exam, and went on to start a business with that website to help others study. The business provided a nice passive income stream on the side.

After Pat got laid off in 2008, he built a business called Smart Passive Income to teach people how to build passive income businesses like he did. His business took off. As more people bought his course, he accumulated a customer base of online business owners.

That business did well in an age when few people were offering similar advice on the internet. As competition emerged, Pat did four things.

First, he emphasized the ethical and proven nature of his approach to differentiate himself from the pack (and, in a shrewd move, to cast doubt on his competitors). He even shared his monthly income online.

Second, Pat leveraged his audience of online business owners to build loyalty and expand his audience. He launched a podcast in July 2010, where customers who had used his system shared their stories.

Third, he developed content about other tactics he has used to build his business to complement his smart passive income course.

Some of the content is free, like his Build Your Own Brand course, further endearing his audience to him and making it easy for new prospects to engage with his brand. Courses like his Power-Up Podcasting©, Amp'd Up Podcasting and 123 Affiliate Marketing command substantial fees. Having proven his worth to this audience and won their loyalty, he is able to charge premium fees relative to other online courses, because his audience loves him and knows the quality of his work.

He wrote a book called *Will It Fly?* to teach owners how to vet their business ideas and another called *Superfans* to teach business owners how to cultivate an enthusiastic audience. Pat has parlayed his expertise, that began with one course, into a suite of helpful tools for his audience of online business owners and aspirants.

Fourth, and most recently, Pat created an opportunity for his community to convene. He hosted a conference, FlynnCon, for them in his hometown of San Diego in July 2019, and plans to make this an annual event.

Pat did all of this by staying close to his audience to hear their needs and creating offerings to meet them. And it paid off for him and his Smart Passive Income brand. Pat's 2017 income (last figure available) was $2,171,652.55.[80]

3. **Attitudinal.** Look for new ways to express or manifest your brand's attitudinal niche. For example, Patagonia's initial mission was "Build the best product, cause no unnecessary harm, use business to inspire and implement solutions to the environmental crisis."[81]

   As more and more sustainable businesses appeared, Patagonia deepened their niche, and not just to compete, but also because the deepening aligned with the values of the company. They expanded their used clothing program, launched a hub to connect customers with environmental activist organizations, and increased their investment in sustainable start-ups. In November 2018, CEO Rose Marcario announced the company would donate the $10 million it received in tax cuts to grassroots environmental organizations.

   In December 2018, Patagonia upped their game on the direction of founder Yvon Chouinard and evolved their mission to, "Patagonia is in business to save our home planet." This statement reasserted their leadership among sustainable businesses.

4. **Geographical.** If your niche is geographical, what can you do to deepen your association with that geography? Do you have competitors from elsewhere invading your territory? Highlight and invest in your position as authentically from the region if that applies.

   Independent bookstores have used geographical niches to thrive in a world where first Barnes & Noble and Borders threatened them, and then Amazon threatened everybody. Independent bookstores like Parnassus Books in Nashville, Tennessee, Powell's in Portland, Oregon and An Unlikely Story in Plainville, Massachusetts build community by hosting book clubs, story times, and author events where patrons can meet their favorite writers and get a signed copy of their book. Their staffs are made up of professional booksellers who make personalized book recommendations. By becoming beloved meeting spots and cultural hubs, they provide benefits Amazon can't dream of.

   Another way to deepen your geographical niche is by the relationships you develop within the community. A client of mine is the only attorney in Kane County, Illinois who does business immigration. As a result, her congressman referred an engineering firm looking for immigration law help to her. She has a wonderful relationship with a renowned lawyer in the area who does family immigration law and they refer clients to each other. Over time, my client has established relationships with universities and companies in the area, emphasizing their ability to meet without a trip to Chicago — and subtly implying without the Chicago overhead. Community location and connections have helped her business grow to take on two full-time staff as well as several part-time helpers.

5. **Product-based, if the product is highly specialized.**
Rather than recoil from the onslaught of competition in the natural snacks industry, owner Stephanie Blackwell drove Aurora Products deeper into the conscientious natural food realm.

At her direction, Aurora has enacted scrupulous cleaning practices drawing accolades from their FDA inspector and achieving Safe Quality Foods superior status in the form of an SQF 2000 Level 3 Certification annually. Other certifications include USDA Organic, Non-GMO Project Verified, Xerces Society's Bee Better and Kosher. Aurora has their own pasteurization system.

The brand has established sustainable environment practices. Aurora Products uses post-consumer RPET packaging which is superior at keeping oxygen out, thus keeping product fresh and 100 percent recyclable. The company also struck a partnership with Newport Biodiesel to deliver 20,000 pounds of used cooking oil to be made into clean-burning biodiesel fuel. This also reduces the amount of petroleum Aurora Products' home state of Connecticut needs to import. Aurora's manufacturing team works with utility companies and closes their plant for a few hours during peak utility usage times to conserve energy.

These conscientious and environmentally friendly efforts appeal to Aurora's customers, endearing the brand further and differentiating it from competitors.

Blackwell also has a plan to invite customers to the plant to see the care, cleanliness, and friendly work environment for themselves. This will further connect customers emotionally to the brand, giving them an experience they are unlikely to have with other vendors.

Today the business, which began as a 100 percent private-label packing anything customers wanted, has evolved into a 35 percent private-label/65 percent Aurora Products brand split of all-natural products only.

6. **Economic.** Walmart deepened their niche as a low-price retailer by incorporating the phrase "Everyday low prices" or EDLP into their advertising, and always focusing on this in campaigns. Yes, I did tell you not to lower your prices at the beginning of this section. Walmart is a rare exception here.

   Walmart executive Jack Shewmaker championed everyday low prices in 1974 to smooth sales curves and increase efficiency as a long-term pricing strategy to build momentum.[82] Shewmaker was codifying a strategy Walmart had followed for most of the company's history, and he added a price-matching policy to back it up.

   Even large companies can take their eyes off their niche and suffer for it. Walmart faltered in 2009 and 2010 when they deviated from their strategy. They had to return to it and double down to counter pressure from Amazon and dollar chains. They trained employees to police prices of competitors and to have competitors' circulars handy to enable easier matching.

   You've worked hard to establish your niche. If competition is challenging your varsity spot in the industry, reassert your niche and fight back!

## To Defend Your Varsity Spot, Stand Taller

And that future basketball star?

The one who loved basketball, grew up south of the Mason-Dixon line, and failed to make the cut the first time he tried out for the high school varsity team?

He was . . . not Michael Jordan.

Did you think I was talking about Michael Jordan?

The guy I was talking about was born in 1984, remember? By that time, Jordan had led the University of North Carolina team to an NCAA Tournament Championship and had been voted NCAA College Player of the Year twice.

No . . . I was talking about Carmelo Anthony.

But they share many similarities. Both were born in Brooklyn. Both had parents who kept them focused on academics. Both missed the cut the first time they tried out for their high school varsity basketball teams. Both worked exceptionally hard after that failure to improve their games.

And . . . both grew several inches before trying out again.

It was the combination of developing new moves, sharpening skills, and height increase that elevated their game and helped them make the team the next time.

If your brand needs to defend its place in your niche, take a page from Mike and Melo. Learn more than your competitors, expand your offerings, sharpen your service, and rise above the pack!

# Key Takeaways from Defending Your Varsity Team Spot

- Brands that need to defend their varsity team spot have seen their niche invaded by many competitors and are finding it increasingly harder to maintain their level of business.

- The need to defend your varsity team spot is inevitable if you were lucky and savvy enough to identify white space for a niche and be alone or one of few doing business in that space. Competitors and opportunists catch on and jump into lucrative markets.

- The best way to defend your niche is to reassert your niche leadership by going deeper into it and reminding your audience of your worth and dedication to them.

- The process of reasserting niche leadership involves a strategic reassessment of your brand to find new ways to serve your audience and provide them with experiences unique to your brand.

# CHAPTER 9

# Oversleeping

## Signs Your Brand Is Oversleeping

If you respond "Yes" to two or more of these questions, your brand may need a wake-up call.

- Has your customer base been slowly shrinking?

- Have you been blindsided by competitors' new products or innovations?

- Do you first learn of competitors' new offerings from their announcements or when they are introduced at trade shows?

- Is your brand scrambling to put together trend-relevant, on-brand products that customers are requesting?

- Have you discovered your customers are buying from competitors to fill gaps in your brand's offering set?

- Is your brand missing a process to collect market and trend data?

- Do you fail to take time regularly to review market and trend data and/or to disseminate that information to your team?

- Are you unable to remember the last time you took time away from the office to review the big picture of your brand and consider your plan for the future?

- Is your brand scrambling to catch up technologically?

- Is outdated technology inviting complaints from customers or employees about your slow-loading website, your website's poor display on mobile phones, or your office systems' inability to keep up with your work pace?

## Dude, Have You Seen My Jacket?

A teenager oversleeps, needs a roommate to wake him, can't find his jacket, and has to borrow a friend's to get out on time.

Sound familiar?

Except this was 17-year-old Red Gerard, Olympian snowboarder from Colorado, on the day he was to compete at the 2018 Winter Olympics in PyeongChang, South Korea.

Even Olympians can't override nature.

# Nature Puts Adolescents on a Different Sleep Schedule

Human adolescents tend to oversleep because the hormonal changes in their bodies delay the release of melatonin, the hormone that makes us sleepy. This delayed release means teens don't get tired until late at night. Still needing eight to ten hours, teens easily sleep until late morning or early afternoon if uninterrupted. When teens oversleep, they are often just following the natural rhythms of their bodies.

This knowledge does not always help parents trying to wake them or get them somewhere on time in the morning. Nor does it excuse the classes, sports practices or other activities they miss as a result. Teens who oversleep regularly miss opportunities and sometimes fall behind.

Brands in adolescence oversleep when they stay with business as usual and ignore developments in their industry that change how the industry operates, what buyers want, and how buyers assess their brand options.

Oversleeping is how Zagat ceded their lead in user-generated restaurant reviews and fell way behind.

## Zagat Has a Groundbreaking Start

When Zagat first launched their namesake restaurant guide in the early 1980s, they were unique. They provided succinct reviews and ratings from patrons instead of critics. This was revolutionary. And, like many revolutionary ideas, it originated from an attempt to solve a problem.

In 1979 Tim and Nina Zagat were out to dinner in New York

City with friends, when one of them complained about a restaurant review in a major newspaper. Tim and Nina suggested that they survey their friends for insights on restaurants, and interviewed 200 of them. The result was a single legal-sized page of restaurant ratings and recommendations that they distributed to their friends and colleagues.

Not long after they began publishing their one-pager, they received a call from a friend who worked at Citibank. The one-pager had landed on his desk with a note at the top that read "To all the officers of the bank." There were 3,000 officers there.

That's when the Zagats decided to commercialize the guide. Publishers resisted their advances in 1982 because they thought the pocket-sized guide — designed to be mobile — would get lost on bookstore shelves. They also resisted the idea that anyone wanted reviews from ordinary people.

But the Zagats knew from their experience that the publishers were failing to see the unmet market need (white space!) and that there would be an audience for the guide.

The Zagats ended up self-publishing what became referred to as the "Burgundy Bible" among New York restaurant goers. Once the guide took off in New York in 1985, they expanded to other cities and began reviewing hotels, specialty retailers, and other services. In sourcing reviews from ordinary people, the Zagats were pioneers of user-generated content. They had the market to themselves for the latter half of the 1980s and most of the 1990s.

Then came the internet.

The couple embraced the internet, collecting survey results online and licensing their content to early web services Prodigy and CompuServe. In 1999, they launched a full-featured website, and two years later, they began charging users to access reviews and ratings. The decision to charge for content was a defensive one — free online content might cannibalize book sales. But the paywall Zagat erected hurt them in two major ways.

First, Google was ascending as the search engine of choice and penalized content behind paywalls in their listings. Zagat was not showing up high on search results. Second, the void at the top of the search results created an environment where free review content like Yelp, Tripadvisor, and Chowhound could flourish.

## Zagat Goes into a Years-Long Slumber

Zagat kept doing the same reviews and hiding them behind a paywall as competitors continued to crowd their niche. This is when Zagat hit their brand adolescence.

I think the Zagats (Nina and Tim) sensed this. I think they hoped their son Ted, who assumed the company presidency in 1999, would take the company to the next level. But he left in 2007.

In 2008, with $40 million in revenue ($30 million from its paper guides), Tim and Nina tried and failed to sell their 29-year-old brand for an asking price of $200 million.[83]

The competitive restaurant review environment made Zagat's investors antsy.

Google bought Zagat in 2011 for $151 million. Marissa Mayer, then vice president of Local, Maps, and Location Services at Google, planned to make Zagat the centerpiece of Google's local search. Within a year, however, Mayer left to head Yahoo. Zagat lost their internal brand champion in the organization. In 2013, Zagat removed the paywall from their website and mobile apps, but by then they had been overtaken by Yelp in traffic and technical prowess.

Over time, Zagat reduced the number of city guides they

printed. The last year they issued guides for major cities that were not New York was 2014, dropping Boston, Chicago, Los Angeles, London, and Paris. Zagat ground to a halt under Google in 2017 when they failed to send out their annual survey, meaning that not even their one remaining guide for New York would be published in 2018.

In early 2018 Google sold Zagat to The Infatuation, a nine-year-old restaurant review company, for an undisclosed sum. The Infatuation sourced restaurant reviews from in-house staff. They intended to keep Zagat separate to capitalize on Zagat's user-generated content appeal, but to apply their tech savvy to the brand.

Because Zagat overslept through the rise of internet restaurant review competition and then languished at Google for years, The Infatuation will have to invest major resources to bring the brand back to relevance and to have current reviews in more than a few cities. The Infatuation team began by recruiting curators in New York in the summer of 2019, printing a 2020 *New York City Guide* in fall 2019. They also conducted research on how people used Zagat in the past and what that might look like in the future. Zagat's future depends on the goodwill and memory of their past fans, and on The Infatuation investing enough to convince them to return and to win over new supporters.

# Good Times and Rigid Thinking Can Lull Your Brand to Sleep

Oversleeping is not based on a single decision a brand team makes, but on adhering to a particular dogma over time. Sometimes the dogma is as simple as "If it's not broke, don't fix it," as evidenced by abundant revenue. It's hard to worry when the money is flowing in. Other times, it is a rigid adherence to traditional business principles that may not apply to a new industry, or on long-held beliefs that at some point became irrelevant.

In Zagat's case, it was at first the lasting insistence that their website reviews needed a paywall to avoid cannibalizing printed guide sales. Later it was the constraints of a disinterested parent company who wanted to mine Zagat's location DNA but did not care about the brand.

But even name recognition can't save a brand that oversleeps too long.

## The Real Story of What Happened to Blockbuster

Blockbuster has become the poster child of the didn't-see-the-disruptor-coming brand community. But that's neither the whole story nor an accurate representation.

Blockbuster opened their first store in 1985 in Dallas, Texas and expanded quickly, launching over 1,000 stores and expanding overseas before being sold to Viacom in 1994 for $8.4 billion. Viacom conducted an initial public offering of Blockbuster stock in 1998 and raised $4.8 billion. The brand continued to open new stores around the world.[84]

Blockbuster was 15 years old in 2000 when Reed Hastings, founder of then three-year-old Netflix, approached their CEO John Antioco and offered to sell Netflix to them for $50 million. At the time, Netflix was offering DVDs for rental by mail. Despite several offers, Antioco declined because he was not convinced consumers would wait for DVDs by mail.

Four years later, after Netflix passed the $500 million annual revenue mark, Antioco was convinced. In August 2004, Blockbuster Online launched their own by-mail DVD service and enticed subscribers by offering free in-store rental coupons. Blockbuster signed up almost as many subscribers in 2004 as Netflix did. They also eliminated late fees.

During a live call with analysts in early 2005, Hastings said, "In the last six months, Blockbuster has thrown everything but the kitchen sink at us." The next day he received a large box from Texas. It contained . . . a kitchen sink.[85]

Antioco's plans to invest in Blockbuster online and to eliminate late fees did not appeal to Viacom which owned 80 percent of Blockbuster's stock. They decided to sell their stake in 2004, which set the stage for notorious investor Carl Icahn to gain a stake, as well as several others.

Once Antioco woke to Netflix's threat, he was not going to let Blockbuster continue oversleeping. He sought to leverage Blockbuster's retail presence against Netflix and launched a program called Total Access in November 2006, allowing customers to return DVDs they had received by mail to any Blockbuster store and receive a free rental.

Total Access let subscribers rent many more movies for their money and soared. By the end of 2006, Blockbuster had 2.2 million subscribers. In early 2007, Netflix lost 55,000 subscribers.

Hastings approached Antioco at the Sundance Film Festival in January 2007 to suggest that Netflix buy Blockbuster Online. Antioco said he would prefer to have the companies merge. A deal never materialized due to antitrust concerns.[86]

Hastings would later admit to Shane Evangelist, former head of Blockbuster Online, that they had had Netflix in checkmate at the time.[87]

It would seem that Blockbuster had turned the tide. But while Antioco was convinced of the path via Blockbuster Online and Total Access, investors disagreed. They lamented forgone income from the halted late fees program. Ultimately, Blockbuster's board got into a compensation dispute with Antioco and forced him out.

The board brought in James Keyes from 7-Eleven as the new CEO. Keyes pulled back on the Total Access program, raised online customers' prices, and refocused on the stores.

From there you can find multiple answers to the question of why Blockbuster failed.

Keyes says Blockbuster failed because the financial crisis in 2008 made it harder to service their $350 million in debt.[88] Jonathan Salem Baskin, a former Blockbuster executive, says the company failed because it began looking at the business like a convenience store, prioritizing sales of movie accompaniments like candy and popcorn above the movies.[89]

I see a company board and investor group trained on short-term profits and failing to understand the industry's evolution, despite the alarm bells Antioco rang. Blockbuster had countered Netflix and was positioned to conquer them when Blockbuster's investors pulled back, giving Netflix unchallenged room to grow and own the streaming space.

Blockbuster never recovered from the strategic pullback. The company declared bankruptcy in September 2010 and closed their last 300 corporate-owned stores in November 2013.

The point of the Blockbuster-Netflix story is that oversleeping for a while won't kill your brand. Like the adolescent who misses some morning classes, you'll have work to do to catch up. But a brand that oversleeps for years and refuses to wake will become the adult child who is never going to leave their parents' basement, and who is never going to be cash-flow positive.

# Dangers of Oversleeping: Loss of Market Leadership, Shrinking Revenues, Bankruptcy

Oversleeping reduces your brand's influence, then its size, and, in the long run, threatens its viability.

At first, oversleeping can look much like needing to defend your varsity team spot. Competitors who have targeted your brand due to its achievements have succeeded in stealing customers and market share. Your brand has fallen behind.

But brands that oversleep fail to heed the early warning signs of losing some customers or having prospects go elsewhere. They rationalize maintaining the status quo because cash is still coming in, because that's what made them successful, or simply because they don't know what to do otherwise. Blockbuster's investors and new leadership under Keyes fell into this category, returning to a prior modus operandi thinking it would still work.

Innovation and market progress keep ticking away, though. Eventually the brand falls so far behind it loses all relevance. How can your brand compete if it's not in the game at all?

It can't. Brands that never wake die.

How do you wake an oversleeping brand before it is too late? You start with a strategic plan.

## Developing Your Strategic Plan

If your brand has been oversleeping, chances are you haven't done strategic planning in a long time — or ever. Maybe not since you started the company.

Daily operations and fire-fighting can easily swallow your

time and make it difficult to step back to look at your brand strategically. But, just as teens aspiring to go to college have to plan to visit and apply, if you want growth to happen you need to plan for it.

Moreover, strategic planning gives your brand a context for operating and decision-making that will make your life easier. Like your brand's purpose, which factors into the process, defining your strategy helps you assess opportunities and actions as being on-strategy or not. A strategic plan also helps you sleep better at night, knowing you have considered both the current marketplace conditions and future opportunities and threats — and have planned to address them.

A well-conceived and executed strategic plan is the remedy to oversleeping and can help prevent oversleeping in the first place.

There are four steps to developing a strategic plan:

1. Understand your position
2. Develop a strategy
3. Make a plan
4. Execute and refine

## 1. Understand Your Position

The process of reviewing and understanding your position in the marketplace is a great antidote to the jarring realization that your brand has been oversleeping. Information and planning counter the unsettling feeling that comes from discovering there are corners of your industry and competitor activity you did not know about.

**Begin by pulling together all the consumer research** you have on your brand and your offerings. If available, have someone glean insights from any online reviews and social media commentary on your brand — the good, the bad, the ugly. You don't wake your brand by protecting it from adverse news. Look for insights on why your audience comes to your brand. What differentiates you from competitors? What does your audience love about your brand? What do they dislike? When do you lose out to your competitors?

**Assemble industry and market data** that give an overview of the size of your industry and who your competitors are — the obvious ones, the upstarts, and everyone in between. What do you know about them?

**Gather employee insights about your brand, your competitors, and your industry.** What can your salespeople and other employees contribute to your organization's competitive and market intelligence? Where does your brand struggle to compete? Where does it shine?

**Conduct a SWOT analysis.** SWOT stands for Strengths, Weaknesses, Opportunities, Threats. Your SWOT analysis is the culmination of this phase and the context for your strategic plan. Invite your management team and employees from different functional areas — marketing, sales, finance, customer service, operations, product development — to participate in this important exercise. Consider including outside advisors or third parties you trust to bring an objective point of view.

For a SWOT analysis to work, it has to be an honest assessment. I recommend having people fill in the SWOT analysis ahead of time and come prepared to share their thoughts. This leads to a more efficient and effective sharing of ideas and more thorough analysis.

Consider asking everyone to generate at least five strengths, weaknesses, opportunities, and threats and to write each one individually on a sticky note. Then you can aggregate the sticky notes and group them by similar sentiment for discussion.

**Strengths and weaknesses are within your control.** These are things you can affect and change. They include your assets, talent, proprietary methods, patents, trademarks, intellectual property, goodwill with customers, customer service, operations, and offerings.

**Strengths are positive attributes internal to your company.**

Questions to help generate strengths:

- What physical assets do you have — equipment, technology, cash, patents, location?

- What intellectual and operational assets do you have on your team — knowledge, expertise, skills, reputation, distribution systems?

- What business processes are successful?

- What relational assets do you have — network connections, customers, vendors, suppliers?

- What do you do really well? Better than anyone else? What competitive advantages do you have?

Among other things, listing and pondering your strengths can also give you a greater appreciation for them. It might also start generating ideas, but jot those to the side and hold off developing them until you have the full SWOT analysis.

**Weaknesses are aspects of your company that detract from your performance.** Customer complaints or service mishap reports can provide insights here.

Questions to help generate weaknesses:

- Are there gaps on your team?

- Are there physical assets that your brand needs — funding, equipment, other?

- Which business processes need improvement?

- Are there quality or delivery issues with your offerings?

- Are there recurring customer-service issues?

- What does your business need to be more competitive — product improvements, more distributors or channels of distribution, a better functioning or updated website?

- Are your sources of supply reliable? Do you have multiple sources or just one?

- Do bottlenecks or out-of-stock situations occur with your inventory?

- Is your location hampering your success?

Once you have done a brand self-assessment via strengths and weaknesses, it's time to look at the world your brand operates in via opportunities and threats.

**Opportunities and threats are aspects of the external environment that could have an impact on your brand.** They are out of your control. You cannot change an opportunity or a threat, you can only seize the former and protect against the latter.

These external forces include consumer trends like shopping habits, health consciousness, and environmental concern; market trends that could make funding more difficult; government regulation and international trade conditions; technology changes and obsolescence; the price of raw materials; and the availability of qualified talent in your workplace's location.

**Opportunities are situations that have evolved in the marketplace that offer your brand a chance to grow in reputation, in sales, in emotional connection with your audience.** Conditions that you don't control, but that can contribute to your brand's success.

Examples of opportunities include:

- A chance to partner with another brand that is a good fit, that serves the same audience, and that would reflect well on your brand.
- A consumer trend that leads new customers to your brand, in the way that environmental concerns are boosting producers of sustainable clothing.
- A conference bringing members of your target audience to your area where your brand could inexpensively exhibit or supply swag.
- Winning an industry award that would enhance your brand's reputation.
- Securing a supply contract that fixes your raw material costs for a determined amount or length of time.

**Threats are situations that have emerged or could emerge that would have a negative impact on your brand.** Preparing to counter or mitigate threats is part of good brand planning and management. Contingency planning beats crisis management every time.

Threats might be:

**Sourcing issues or vulnerabilities.** How vulnerable are you to a price increase for your raw materials? What would happen if there was a shortage? Or if one of your sources missed a delivery?

**New market entrants.** How might their entrance affect your brand?

**New technology** that could render your product obsolete or make it less effective.

**Changes in consumer behavior** due to worries about the economy, or an evolution in the way consumers shop.

**Unfavorable trends.** Is your market shrinking due to consumer, technological or other trends? Newspapers, fax machines, and the beef industry have all faced this kind of threat. Bottled water companies which saw consumption rise for decades are now facing a strong backlash against plastic bottles. Keeping brands going in the face of these kinds of threats can be a daunting task and requires planning.

**Unfavorable legislation.** The Clorox Company's Glad brand has had to contend with plastic bag bans in many municipalities, US states, and countries. Their response has included reducing the amount of plastic in some of their bags, offering biodegradable bags, and supporting multiple sustainable initiatives such as sponsoring reuse events where toys, coats, and electronic devices are transferred to people in need of those items.

| SWOT Analysis for:_____ | |
|---|---|
| Strengths (areas where your company excels, within your control) | Opportunities (marketplace developments or external forces that offer your brand a chance to advance) |
|  |  |
| Weaknesses (internal performance detractors, within your control) | Threats (marketplace developments or external forces that could hinder or damage your brand) |
|  |  |

Pull your analysis together for your company on one sheet, and then do another sheet for each major competitor.

After you have completed your SWOT analysis, use this context to determine your brand positioning if you have not already, or to reaffirm or tweak it.

Brand positioning is a long-lasting brand component, not something that changes frequently. As such it might require you to pause the strategic planning process here to develop your positioning. It involves iterations and consumer research, and may take weeks to finalize.

Brand positioning statements express what your brand does for whom and why [the benefit], including your brand's unique ability to deliver your offerings. If you already have your purpose, attributes, audience, and niche defined, you may have the components of your positioning already and just need to put them together and confirm them.

Here are some examples of brand positioning statements. Because positioning statements are for internal use only, I have written them based on research, but have not gotten them directly from the companies.

**Simple Bank:** Simple Bank provides online banking for consumers who want a simpler, more transparent bank and effortless personal financial management. Simple Bank offers an all-in-one platform with no fees backed by personalized customer service.

**Gluten Free Territory** (featured in Chapter 6): Gluten Free Territory provides premium gluten-free desserts for consumers who want to eat gluten-free without sacrificing any aspect of their dessert experience. Gluten Free Territory has perfected their recipes to ensure each product delivers the look, aroma, mouthfeel, and taste it should, and tests all products to fewer than five parts per million of gluten.

**Constant Contact:** Constant Contact helps small businesses and non-profits succeed by providing marketing tools that help them build and deepen customer relationships. Constant Contact brings deep and current technological expertise to offer an all-in-one marketing solution, local learning and coaching opportunities, and customer service from real people.

Don't be fooled by the simplicity of these statements. Simplicity is key so that your entire organization can remember your brand positioning, execute it, and take pride in it.

## 2. Develop strategies

One you have confirmed your positioning and have your SWOT analysis handy, it's time to use the analysis to develop strategies that leverage your strengths, mitigate your weaknesses, and deepen your market position. You may include specific strategies to help your brand recover from oversleeping, strategies to catch up in your industry or leap forward.

A strategy is a method of how your brand will approach your market and grow. It doesn't come out of the blue, but is tied to your niche and the market you serve.

To brainstorm strategies, review your SWOT and consider questions like:

How can your strengths help seize opportunities? How can they counter threats?

How can your opportunities combat your weaknesses and mitigate threats?

What opportunities do you spot in the marketplace that your competitors have missed or that are best suited to your strengths?

If a new audience or niche is on your radar for growth, develop strategies that leverage your strengths to reach them.

Examples of strategies:

- We will educate our customers on the breadth of our offerings to generate more repeat business.

- We will cross-train salespeople on all our products so that one salesperson can handle all of a customer's needs, streamlining the company's relationship with the customer and allowing the salesperson to deepen the relationship on the company's behalf.

- We will have several brand team members attend trade shows related to our newly identified niche to jumpstart our relationships in that niche and to help the entire team get up to speed.

You are better off executing fewer strategies well than generating lots that peter out before they come to fruition. After you brainstorm strategies, prioritize between 1-4 of them to grow your business depending on your resources (staff size, funding, space, etc.).

# 3. Make a plan

While you need an idea of where your brand is going long-term, I'm not a fan of making detailed plans for more than a year or two at a time, unless an initiative requires a longer timeframe. The world moves too fast and, invariably, unforeseen events change priorities.

For your strategies to produce results though, you need a plan. This will specify how your strategies will be executed. Plans should detail your goals, the timing, who is accountable for the activities, and the source and amount of budget available.

Formulate goals using the SMART (Specific, Measurable, Achievable, Relevant, Time-bound) guidelines to describe exactly what will happen. For example, in relation to the strategy above to educate customers on the breadth of services available, your goal might be a biweekly customer newsletter.

- **S**pecific: Start an entertaining newsletter that demonstrates your brand's expertise and that mentions the corresponding services or products once every fifth edition.

- **M**easurable: Biweekly (once every two weeks).

- **A**chievable: Our marketing communications group will make this a priority and has the talent, time, and budget to follow through.

- **R**elevant: The content should use the brand's voice, be mindful to emphasize the brand's attributes, and contain information that interests, entertains, and informs customers.

- **Time-bound:** Every other Tuesday.

Once you have your goals, spell out the timing, accountability, and budget for each one. Perhaps you have a marketing communications manager who will assume this responsibility, taking a month to get the newsletter set up (uploading contacts, formulating a template, developing an editorial calendar for the newsletter) and then begin publishing in week six of the plan.

Your budget will need to cover the cost of an email service provider. Depending on your industry, you might also want to put an allocation toward purchasing images or hiring a professional photographer and a graphic designer if you do not have one on staff.

Your strategic plan should begin with an understanding of the industry and your position, and then include goals, timing, accountability, and budget for each strategy you plan to implement. This does not need to be a document of encyclopedic thickness. In fact, I favor streamlined plans that tell it like it is and are easy to share among all involved in executing them.

## 4. Execute and Refine

The beauty of having a plan with well-detailed goals and timing is that it takes the big thinking out of your everyday life and makes it easier to include the incremental activities you need to achieve your goals on your daily to-do list. Harness the power of your strategic plan by scheduling right into your calendars the tasks you and your team need to accomplish to realize your goals.

Having those tasks present frequently also helps keep your brand awake. Remember that you formulated your strategic plan to remedy or prevent oversleeping.

If you have created a good plan, your challenge will now be to execute the tasks on time and not push them off when unforeseen issues or activities arise. Great brands move forward not in quantum leaps, but in the day-to-day adherence to their long-term goals. That's what the individual tasks that work toward your strategic goals are. They are the road to brand growth, and are every bit as important as your routine tasks. They need to become part of your routine.

Most brands can thrive with an annual strategic planning process. Unless your brand is technologically driven, reviewing the state of your industry and the position of the players once a year is enough. Tech industry brands might do this every six months.

This is not to say things won't change between strategic planning sessions. They will. Take care not to let little changes in the industry or shiny new competitive products derail you from the solid thinking you did for your brand. Stick to your plan unless something major merits a change in priorities.

Don't wait an entire year to measure your progress, though. Depending on your goals, have monthly or quarterly check-ins to ensure progress is happening on schedule and that those accountable have what they need to help you grow your brand.

## Strategic Planning Saves Brands and Helps Them Flourish

Erin Calvo-Bacci, owner of CB Stuffer which we talked about in Chapter 6, used strategic planning to bring her brand back from the brink and to discover her niche. "In 2009 we were a wink away from dead." — Erin Calvo-Bacci

It was through a strategic, big-picture look at her brand that Erin and her husband Carlo discovered the manufacturing side was carrying the business and that the retail side, The Chocolate Truffle, was bleeding funds. In SWOT parlance, manufacturing was their strength and retail was a weakness.

Erin's savvy look at trends helped her realize that recent Massachusetts legislation precluded medical device companies from sending perks or gifts to buyers. Medical device buyers had constituted a large portion of her corporate clients, and this legislation resulted in a massive cut in business, forcing her to look elsewhere for customers. The legislation was a threat to her business that became real.

She also saw that consumer trends meant online shopping was growing while retail foot traffic was down. "People [were] not walking around, not walking into little Mom and Pop stores as much as 10 years ago. Foot traffic was way down," Erin told me. Selling online was an opportunity for the brand.

Erin's strategic plan used Bacci Chocolate Design's strengths as a foundation, their unique peanut butter cup as a niche, and her trend observations to close her brick-and-mortar outlets and concentrate on wholesale and online selling. It is also what ultimately lead her to change the name of the company to CB Stuffer. And it set the brand on a path to success.

## From Slumber to Success

Despite oversleeping, Red Gerard, the 17-year-old US Olympian snowboarder, made it to his event on time. He was in last place going into his third and final run, but rallied and won the United States' first gold medal at the 2018 Winter Olympics.

Not all oversleeping stories end this well. The key here is that someone woke Red. He needed an external force to bring him to consciousness and get him going.

If your brand in adolescence is oversleeping, it will be up to you to wake it by conducting an industry analysis, putting together a strategic plan, and executing it.

# Key Takeaways from Oversleeping

- Brands oversleep when they ignore industry and marketplace developments for periods of time, falling behind in their offerings and losing customers.

- Short periods of oversleeping force brands to play catch-up, while long periods can ultimately kill your brand.

- The way to wake an oversleeping brand is by conducting an industry analysis, formulating a strategic plan, and executing it.

- Robust industry analyses include SWOT analyses which are profiles of the strengths, weaknesses, opportunities, and threats facing your brand and your competitors.

- The key to keeping a brand awake and growing is to pay attention to the industry, follow through on a well-conceived strategic plan and not forgo the day-to-day tasks involved in achieving plan goals.

# CHAPTER 10

# Asserting Independence

## Signs Your Brand is Asserting Independence

If you answer "Yes" to two or more of these questions, your brand might be signaling a readiness to leave your nest.

- Are you feeling burned out?

- Do you dread going to work or meetings?

- Is your brand experiencing high turnover?

- Are you having trouble securing funding for your brand?

- Do you yearn for the way things were in the early years of the company?

- Do you hate interviewing and hiring?

- Does your brand have long-standing unfilled positions or gaps in expertise?

- Do you feel like you are out of ideas for your brand?

- Do small issues often pop up and get out of control?

## License to Direct Your Own Life

Several of my teenage memories recall disagreements and negotiations with my parents over my curfew. Until the middle of my senior year in high school my parents insisted I be home by midnight. Most of my friends were a year or two older. None of them had such an early curfew.

I made such a stink on my 17th birthday — when I got my driver's license — that my parents relented. "Okay, 12:30 am," they said. I rolled my eyes. I still had the earliest curfew.

The strange thing is that I didn't always want to be out later than 12:30 am. But I wanted to be the one to decide when I came home.

Curfews may be small change in the scheme of life.

But the decision of whether to stay in college or join the NBA? Bigger stakes there.

## Take the Money Now or Stay in School

While I was arguing curfews with my parents in Fair Lawn, New Jersey in 1981, basketball player Jason Williams was starting life 36 miles away in the town of Plainfield.

Williams' family had a strong belief in education. Both of his parents went to college. His mother Althea went on to get two master's degrees, finishing the second while Jason was in college. When Jason's basketball game tape impressed Coach Mike Krzyzewski at Duke University, they must have been thrilled. Duke had a reputation for basketball players who graduated before joining the NBA.

Anyone who follows US college basketball knows who Mike Krzyzewski is. Krzyzewski has been the head coach of Duke University's men's basketball team since 1980. In that time, the team has won 15 ACC Championships, been to 12 Final Fours and won five NCAA tournament National Championships.

Krzyzewski's love for college basketball led him to turn away numerous NBA head coach opportunities, including offers from the Boston Celtics in 1990 and the Los Angeles Lakers in 1994.[90]

Williams respected and liked Coach K, as Krzyzewski is known, but he admits to not understanding Coach K's thinking and approach while he was there and getting angry at him for the intensity he threw at him.

In hindsight, Williams writes in his memoir, *Life is Not an Accident: A Memoir of Reinvention*, it was Coach K's insight into who Williams was and how he played that prompted him to yell and antagonize him.

"Looking back, I get it: K pushed my buttons because he knew I played better when I was angry. I don't know when he figured that out — maybe from watching me in high school or from observing how I responded to his various motivational efforts during my freshman year. Who knows? What I do know is we won a national championship, and I became a two-time national player of the year."[91]

In his sophomore year, Williams led Duke to their NCAA Basketball Championship win in April 2001, breaking the Duke record for number of points scored in one season and leading the ACC league in scoring. A standout year by any measure. And a moment to consider joining the NBA draft.

Clearly the expectation from Williams' parents would be that he would stay in school. And with Duke's reputation for graduates, Williams expected Coach K to tell him to stay when he sought his advice.

But that's not what happened.

Instead, Williams writes in his memoir, he and Coach K had "one of the most eye-opening conversations" of his life, weighing pros and cons. Williams recalls,

"At the end of it, he said, 'You know, Jay. You have to make whatever decision that's best for you and your family, whatever is in your best interest to grow as a human being and a man. But I dare you to be different. I dare you not to follow the norm. You always talk about wanting to be a pioneer. Well here's your chance to blaze your own path.'

"I left that room thinking on those words for a while. All of a sudden I thought, 'I don't want to be the norm.' The norm would've been to take the easy way out and to leave. I made the decision to stay in school.

"However my life worked out, even if I didn't get hurt, that was the best decision I ever made my entire life. That was a decision that was bigger than basketball. It was a decision about me wanting to better myself. I will be forever indebted to him for not telling me what to do, but for giving me the options and showing me how things could positively or negatively impact me. I look at him every day and say, 'Thank you, man. Thank you.'"[92]

Why did Coach K not tell Williams what to do? He knew to respect Williams' desire to make his own decision. Even though Williams ended up making the same decision as his parents would have supported, Coach K had the skill, the credibility, and the approach to help him grow as a person in making that decision.

# When Adolescents Assert Independence

Asserting independence is a key component of adolescence.

In psychology, this is known as the second separation-individuation and is credited to Peter Blos, who identified the stage as one where an adolescent needs to establish a self that is separate, distinct, and individual. (Margaret Mahler identified the first separation-individuation as occurring during the first years of life.)

If you have parented teenagers, you know it as the time period beginning at the end of elementary school or in middle school when your children suddenly become much less interested in sharing their day or being with you and much more interested in their friends. You shift from being in complete control of their schedule and activities to being happy to know where they are and having some idea of what they are up to.

Making this transition requires a parent to move from a control mindset to one akin to a coach. A coaching mindset educates and directs with the aim of having the coachee make good decisions and perform well in the moment. Some parents transition well to this phase. Others find it difficult.

In separating from their parents, adolescents sometimes look to other adults in their life for guidance. Teachers, coaches, guidance counselors, and other community members may have expertise in a teen's interest or have earned their trust. Consulting these other adults is an act of independence. It helps teens gain knowledge and skills that may be beyond their parents' purview.

While parents may feel saddened or disappointed not to be

consulted, they can also feel relieved, especially if they have confidence in the person their adolescent has chosen for guidance.

# When Brands Assert Independence

If you are the founder of your business, you have a similar trajectory. As a start-up and early-stage company, you hired people to execute your vision and had a hand in every decision.

If your brand has had success, though, at some point it will become impossible for you to be that present, nor might you be interested in every little decision. Meetings start to take up most of your day.

Some founder-leaders are okay with that and have the skills to shift from vision provider to executer, but not all do. Some are interested in running the day-to-day operations, others aren't.

## Life is Good Starts Slow, Then Soars

Life is Good's origins began in 1989 when the founders, brothers Bert and John Jacobs, were in their early 20s. Eager to sell their artwork and avoid "real jobs," they founded Jacobs Gallery and began selling T-shirts on the street in the Boston area as a way to market their designs. They struggled to stay afloat. After five years of barely squeaking by and living in a van, they got jobs as substitute teachers and finally rented an apartment.

Continuing their dream, they would regularly post their designs on the wall of their apartment and poll friends for feedback. An early version of Jake, a crudely drawn smiling stick figure, inspired a friend to write "This guy has life figured out." Later they posted 50 potential slogans on the wall and "life is good" drew a similarly positive reaction.

Combining the slogan and Jake on a T-shirt, they printed 48 test tees which sold out in 45 minutes at a fair in Cambridge, Massachusetts in 1994. They would go on to gross $82,000 that year.[93]

They hit on the idea of infusing their desire to spread optimism through their work and founded Life is Good. Thanks to the faith of, and exposure from, a few early retailers, sales hit $260,000 in 1996 and $2 million in 1998. After trademarking the brand, hiring more people, and getting warehouse space, the brand continued to soar, reaching $100 million and 200 employees in 2007.

## Revenues Hit $100 Million · · · and Stay There

After years of 30 percent growth, it slowed in 2008 to 10 percent and then plateaued for years. Not for lack of ambition, though. The brothers tried a couple of different approaches to get growth going.

In 2014 Bert told *Fortune* magazine, "We're going to become more of a media and communications company. Apparel is just where it started. We can become a billion-dollar company driving positive social change, teaching, and reinforcing the values we think are most important in the world."[94]

In 2015, Bert announced a new approach to relaunch the business, dubbed the "Arthouse Strategy," accompanied by a logo change. The Arthouse Strategy aimed to attract new, younger customers by opening product design and marketing to designs from many artists — painters, sculptors, animators, filmmakers, poets, and dancers — supporting art the way the Jacobs brothers had hoped to sell their designs in the beginning. Their intent was good, but the strategy did not budge revenues.

# Do You Want to Be Rich or King?

Like parenting, leading a business requires different skill sets at different stages. To succeed you need to understand the skills your brand needs at the helm of each stage and provide them yourself, get help, or step aside. Other reasons business founders and owners find the brand has outgrown them include that they are burned out, they lack the knowledge needed to get the resources the brand needs, or they simply have grappled with the same problems repeatedly and don't know how to solve them.

In a humble moment, the leader might also ask if they have the support of the organization to continue.

Dodging these questions and not periodically assessing whether you are still equipped to lead your brand can have dire consequences, or at least handicap your brand.

Noam Wasserman, a Harvard Business School professor for 13 years and now dean of Yeshiva University's Sy Syms School of Business, described the decision of whether the founder should continue to lead an organization as "The Founder's Dilemma" in a *Harvard Business Review* article in February 2008. For self-aware business founders, the decision is not stay or go, but comes earlier in the form of: do I want to be "rich or king?"

Wasserman's extensive research into the decisions that founders make and how they affect the founder's companies showed that they rarely got both.

Founders whose inspiration focused on making money tended to leave their companies. Even before leaving, they were likely to share equity with co-founders and key employees. At the point where their company outgrew their management skills, they stepped aside. Self-aware founders did this on their own. Many others hung on until forced out by boards or venture capital firms.

Founders whose primary desire was to lead an organization took less outside funding and grew their companies more slowly to remain in control. They earned less than their monetarily focused counterparts both in the moment and overall. But they remained at the helm of their companies.

In a 2015 CNBC interview with Life is Good's Bert Jacobs, renowned businessman Marcus Lemonis talked about the tough decision that occurs when you bring in new leadership as also being a decision that balances ego and longevity. Lemonis commented,

> *When is the right time for the founder to sort of step aside and know that there is somebody better? And so you see this sort of dichotomy between ego and longevity. And ego usually ends up in the grave. And the longevity of being able to be humble about it is telling investors or customers that we don't have all the answers. And I think it can work. And more importantly I think it's necessary. And I think about it even in my own businesses.*[95]

We've already seen the detriment to businesses where founders and business owners stayed too long.

In Chapter 9 with Zagat, I'm betting that the Zagats' son left the business in 2007 because his parents were too heavy-handed in directing the brand or he felt he did not have the skills to do it. If instead of desperately looking to sell, Nina and Tim Zagat had acknowledged they had taken the business as far as they could and had sought the right new leader, perhaps the brand would not have languished or required a fire sale to satisfy investors.

Segway founder Dean Kamen also waited too long to step aside, as we saw in Chapter 5.

If this whole idea seems upsetting to you, but you suspect this may apply to your situation, you should know that with the right approach many business owners have made this transition successfully and have gone on to be happier, not to mention richer.

## Why Reid Hoffman Stepped down as LinkedIn CEO

Reid Hoffman was the founder of LinkedIn, and CEO for their first five years. Hoffman loved the early stages of building the company which involved devising strategies, innovative problem-solving, and developing technologies. As LinkedIn grew, though, he saw the nature of the CEO role changing,

> *At 50 people and beyond, a CEO increasingly has to focus on process and organization, and that wasn't what I was passionate about. For example, I didn't like running a weekly staff meeting. I could do it, but I did so reluctantly, not enthusiastically. I'd rather be solving intellectual challenges and figuring out key strategies, not debating which employees should get a promotion or configuring project timelines.*[96]

This insight, which came just two years into LinkedIn's existence in 2005, incited Hoffman to replace himself as CEO. He hired Dan Nye in early 2007, handing the mantle to him and keeping the product development piece for himself. Nye doubled the size of the company by building a sales department and rebuilding the executive team.

Two years in though, Hoffman realized that the CEO needed to own the product strategy piece as well. He stepped back in as CEO to helm the company while he sought a candidate with consumer internet product experience. Jeff Weiner fit the bill, and became CEO in 2009. Weiner orchestrated the sale of the company to Microsoft in 2016 and continued to lead as CEO until June 2020 when he handed the reins to Ryan Roslansky.

Hoffman's advice to CEOs, "In my experience, CEOs need to derive satisfaction from the nuts and bolts of building a company, not just building product and articulating the vision. They need to be passionate about leadership, management, and organizational processes as the company scales."[97]

Hoffman became executive chairman of LinkedIn's board when Weiner became CEO, and purposefully traveled for much of the first several months of Weiner's tenure to help the LinkedIn organization get used to going to Weiner for decisions. Post-travel, Hoffman became a partner in venture capital firm Greylock Partners. He still consulted with and advised Weiner on occasion, but focused on his board seats representing Greylock at firms like Airbnb and Coda.

## Why Clay Collins Stepped down as Leadpages CEO

Sometimes it's not just that the founder does not enjoy the operational aspects of growing a company, but that they lack the skills to scale it.

This isn't exactly what Clay Collins said in his candid post on July 27, 2017 in which he announced that John Tedesco would succeed him as CEO of Leadpages. Instead, he referenced Reid Hoffman's post and said he was not as passionate about the process and organization aspects of the CEO role that come about after a company tops the 100-employee mark. But the message was there between the lines:

*During our rapid growth, the CEO role has shifted dramatically, and I wanted to pass the baton to someone with scaling in their DNA. . . .*

*I'm really proud of what we've accomplished since Tracy, our technical cofounder Simon Payne, and I founded Leadpages in January of 2013. We've grown to 175 people and $25 million in recurring revenue . . . We have over 46,000 paying customers and have raised $38 million in funding. . . .*

*All in all, I think I'm a pretty good $0-$20M startup CEO. But we're well beyond that now and it's time to have the scaling dude in the seat to take us to $100M+. And that dude is John Tedesco. . . .*

*I might someday be the guy to take a company all the way to $100 million, but for this company (my first software company), that won't be me.*[98]

I admired Collins' humility and candor. There is nothing wrong with playing to your entrepreneurial strengths and leaving the scaling to professional CEOs. I also loved what he said about promoting Tedesco from COO to CEO, "When executed properly, promotions simply label what someone is already doing and empower them to double down on their genius. And that's exactly what this is."

Leadpages was four and a half years old when Collins transitioned the CEO role to Tedesco. Collins was in his mid-30s at the time and had 13-month-old twin girls. Like Hoffman, he reduced his time at work. He still contributed to high-level strategy and product discussions, and still represented Leadpages (and recently purchased ecommerce firm, Drip) on podcasts and webinars and at conferences. He became board chairman at Drip, and launched Nomics just two months after he promoted Tedesco.

The CEO transition happened at a young age for LinkedIn and Leadpages because they are technically driven companies. You can think of technical brand years like dog years. Non-tech industry companies take longer to develop and grow, and that's not a bad thing. It's just how it happens. For that reason, founders may be able to run the company much longer before running into the need to shift skill sets to scale the company, maybe 10-25 years.

At some point though, every brand hits a junction where the organization needs more structure and process definition to continue to grow effectively.

# Dangers of Asserting Independence: Operational Strains, Low Morale, Financial Handicapping, Damage to Brand Reputation, and CEO Unhappiness

Brands in adolescence that are asserting their independence hit a sales or other operational plateau, just like other brands in adolescence. For these brands though, if the skill set to scale is missing, management's response is often to ask employees to work longer and harder than they already are. A lack of effort from employees may not be the problem though, so this pressure strains the firm's operations, as it fails to lift sales or production.

Sustained over time, that pressure and the long hours demanded will also depress employee morale, as they feel the brunt of the brand's struggles without being empowered to help by leadership who can assist them in scaling the brand. Some employees will leave. If the business owner and top management don't enjoy recruiting, interviewing, and hiring, those positions may remain unfilled which, in turn, strains operations and the remaining employees even more.

Another management reaction to the plateau will be to try to invest in more — more production, more employees, more of whatever they think will lift the sales needle. As the brand's revenues continue to strain, the company might seek outside funding for initiatives that management believes will solve the problem. Investors might look at the intent the firm has for the funding, the brand's current position, and the leadership and see the lack of skills to scale. They may deny funding or require new leadership before granting it.

Employees who have left, as well as those who remain, may share their frustrations and disappointment with the brand with their friends and family. As that information travels, the brand may gain a reputation as not being a good place to work. High-caliber candidates who have done their homework may not be interested once they hear this. Fewer candidates may consider employment there. Talent acquisition will then take longer and cost more.

Perhaps most tragically, the business founder/owner no longer enjoys leading the business. They feel burned out, unhappy, and frustrated. This makes them less fun to be around and less effective at leading. It also diminishes the owner's quality of life.

This can be a painful notion for business owners to consider. Sometimes time away from the office helps bring perspective.

## A Road Trip Helps Life Is Good Find the Path Forward

In June 2015, Bert and John Jacobs hired Lisa Tanzer as head of marketing. Lisa was a Harvard Business School graduate who had two decades of experience working in marketing and strategy for consumer brands including Hasbro, Staples, and Gillette. She had also been on the Life is Good Foundation board since their inception, so she was a friend of Bert and John.

Lisa set in motion a number of purpose-related initiatives for the brand, such as establishing strategic partnerships with like-minded non-profit and for-profit organizations and a nationwide Life is Good tour to raise money for kids in need. For the tour, John and Bert went back on the road in their van to talk to customers. Over eight weeks they traveled 3,000 miles, stopping in 40 communities and raising over $1 million through their #GrowtheGood campaign.

In a CNBC interview with Marcus Lemonis and Tyler Mathisen on November 11, 2015, Bert talked about how the trip got them back in touch with customers and gave them ideas on how to grow the brand. He described a strategy shift they were trying to effect — and it was not the Arthouse Strategy he had announced just months earlier. Instead, Bert talked about moving from an apparel company to "a hub of optimism, a place people can go to get good news, to share good news, to share good stories, to feel good about being a human being. It's as much about emotional wellness as anything."[99]

He also shared that he and John had decided that they needed new leadership to grow the brand further.

> While I think that we've been good founders to get from A to B, we're really not the operators to take this from $100 million to a billion plus. And we think somebody else can.
>
> The timeless elements of the brand have little to do with my brother and I. Our strategy is to bring in talent that's smarter, faster, more experienced than we are. We'll still play a role as founders of the business and as creative talent on the team.

*But we have no ego about being the ones running the business. We're going to bring in somebody. So we are looking for a president right now.*

In July 2016, Bert and John promoted Lisa to president of Life is Good. The brand's revenues are still being reported as $100 million, but Lisa has led the brand deeper into their purpose of spreading the power of optimism. Initiatives have included funding research on optimism, hiring an optimism expert, and launching the #SomethingGood campaign in the spring of 2019.

Bert and John are still very involved in the company, but are now able to focus on what they do best — working on the creative aspects and spreading their message of optimism. In April 2019 they gave live interviews with local television news and talk shows around the country about the optimism research, why optimism is important, and publicizing the #SomethingGood campaign. Like #GrowingtheGood, #SomethingGood again raised $1 million for kids by donating one dollar for every story shared to the campaign.

From a brand component standpoint, Life is Good has it good. The brand's purpose — to spread the power of optimism — is clear and succinct, and doubles as an awesome attitudinal niche. Life is Good calls their values "superpowers" and has spelled them out to their organization, on their website, and in Bert and John Jacobs' 2015 book *Life is Good: The Book*. Life is Good's brand voice consistently comes across as realistic, compassionate, and upbeat. And the brand knows its audience. "People who are facing adversity embrace our message the most," Bert Jacobs says.[100]

Life is Good is going long and deep into their niche to grow, focusing on reaching more of their core audience, their most enthusiastic supporters — people facing adversity. Which, if you think about it, is a large swath of the population. Who among us hasn't had a moment when we felt the world was harsh, that we were facing an uphill battle, and were looking for hope?

The founders realizing they were best suited for spreading the message, telling the brand story and continuing their creative roles, but not running the business was a huge step, and is probably the linchpin that will finally move their annual revenue above the $100 million mark.

## Deciding If You Should Step Aside

Brands that are asserting their independence are highlighting a leadership problem — lack of skills to scale, a lack of interest in management (vs. entrepreneurial or other activities) or some other factor inhibiting their ability to grow the brand further. The solution for these brands is often having the leader step aside and promoting or finding new leadership.

How do you know if you should step aside and find a new leader for your brand?

This can be a painful question for business owners to consider.

The answer requires a hard and honest look at your motives for starting the company, factored against the condition of the company today. If you are experiencing burnout, dread, or some of the other warning signs mentioned at the beginning of the chapter, perhaps it's time for you to revisit what you want to get out of your company.

As a first step, think back to your founding. What motivated you? Answer Noam Wasserman's founder's dilemma: did you want to be rich or king? Were you seeking money or control and leadership of an organization?

Next consider the questions LinkedIn founder Reid Hoffman advises asking yourself:[101]

"What am I focused on?"
"What am I world-class at?"
"What am I really committed to?"

Write down your answers. Writing forces you to clarify your thoughts. Step away once you are done and review your answers later. Are they the answers you would want to see from a candidate looking to lead your brand?

Another avenue to think this through might be to collect some data. When I was making a strategic shift in my business, tracking my time helped bring new insights. For 10 business days, track your activities in 15-minute increments.

At the end of the period, look at your days. How are you spending your time? What aspects of leading are you enjoying? What do you dread?

If you are still enjoying your time at your company and are committed to remaining there, but lack the skills for your brand's stage of growth, your task should be to find ways to develop the skills you need. Executive coaching, executive MBA programs, management consultants, and CEO peer groups are all resources that can help you recommit to your business by improving your ability to lead it.

If you find yourself spending the majority of your time on necessary activities that you dislike or have trouble with, this may be a signal that a role change could make you happier and improve the business.

Can you envision yourself taking a role in the company, but not leading it? Is there an area you love that you'd prefer to focus on? For Bert and John Jacobs, those areas are the creative aspect of the brand and spreading the message of optimism. They did not mind giving up the day-to-day running of the business to focus on these.

The hard truth is that if the CEO job is no longer fulfilling you, or if you lack the skills your brand needs to grow and aren't interested in developing them, your brand would benefit from a new CEO. This will only work if you are fully on board with the change and willing to let the new CEO lead without interfering or diluting their authority.

## Recruiting a New CEO

If you decide you are ready to cede the role of leader or you need to get the right skill set in place for your brand's next phase of growth, the next steps are to talk to your board and begin recruiting.

Optimally, you would do this before you are burned out or your brand is in trouble, leaving time for you to bring your successor in and prepare them. With or without that time luxury, there are three key steps to transition a new CEO successfully into your brand.

1. Recruit the right person.
2. Ensure the new leader has your confidence.
3. Ensure the new leader gains the confidence of your organization.

To recruit the right person, begin by writing a job description.

Run the description by trusted advisors, ideally other business owners, to get their perspective and objective opinions.

Next, you want to decide whether to hire from outside the company or to promote from within. Your job description will help you assess viable candidates. If you have time to bring someone in and prepare them, or if you have a good internal candidate, that's great. Hopefully you have seen that person in a managerial capacity before and know they have the sensitivity needed to thrive in your culture, as well as the skills to lead your brand.

When looking at internal candidates, you'll want to answer these questions:

- If I have been distracted or struggling to lead, has someone naturally stepped into the leadership role?

- If so, are they doing well?

- Does their skill set match the brand's needs?

- Do they have the confidence of the organization?

- Do they have the expertise and experience?

If you hire from outside, you'll want to ensure that person is a good fit with your brand culture and can do the job before making them CEO. You can interview and hire someone for a lower position (but maybe still C-suite) with the understanding that they may take over your role if they prove a good fit first. This means giving them a high-level role to see how they fare.

## Transitioning Successfully

Once you have identified your successor and are confident you have the right person, you need to transition carefully. Their successful assent to CEO depends on your expressing your full confidence in them, spelling out what your role will be, if any, and then supporting these statements with your actions. It could involve following the footsteps of Reid Hoffman and Clay Collins by spending a lot of time out of the office in the first few months of the transition to habituate employees to seek the new CEO to answer questions and make decisions.

If you choose to stay around, you will need to resist making decisions that are the purview of the CEO, instead directing employees to your successor. Both out of the office and in, the transition will involve patience on your part so your employees develop a relationship with the new CEO and the habit of consulting them for decision-making. This patience can be emotionally trying, so even if you decide to stay, spending less time in the office for a while as your new CEO establishes themself is a good idea.

In addition to the excitement of taking the burden of the brand off your back, bringing in a new CEO gives you the time and space to consider what you want to do next. Do you have a pet project or cause? An idea for a new business? Do you want more time personally to pursue passions and to spend with family? Considering what you want as early as possible in the process will give you a direction to take as your new CEO settles in.

## The Right Coach Makes All the Difference

Coach K loves working with adolescents. He knows how to relate to them and guide them to success, as evidenced in his provoking Jason Williams to get him to play his best game. To Krzyzewski, it is all about building long-term relationships, both with the players and among them through shared experience. In his memoir, Jason Williams wrote about how at Duke the basketball team was family, that Coach K insisted on it, with older players looking out for the younger ones.[102]

Whether you are a fan of his or not, it is clear Krzyzewski has the skills and know-how to promote player growth. He proved to be the right coach and guide for Williams, not just for basketball but for life.

After his memorable conversation with Coach K, Williams stayed one more year at Duke. He finished his coursework to graduate in three years, and was the second pick of the 2002 NBA draft, going to the Chicago Bulls. He changed his name from Jason to Jay to avoid confusion with two other NBA players at the time.

Only 21 years old, Williams was still an adolescent when he started with the Bulls.

He did not find the leadership or support on the team that he had with Coach K. The average age of the players was 23, meaning his arrival spelled competition to others who viewed him as a threat to their playing time and stats. That mentality probably had something to do with the losses the team strung up that year. Coming from Duke, Williams was not used to losing and not used to teammates who did not care.

He still wanted to exercise his growing independence in some way, and expressed it by buying a motorcycle.

"I had worked hard to become an NCAA champion, a two-time national player of the year, and the second pick of the draft, and yet I had this team of people around me always telling me what I should or shouldn't be doing. I wanted — no, I needed — to make my own decisions, to have some control over my own life. The Yamaha R6 symbolized that for me."[103]

Lacking camaraderie with his Bulls' teammates, he found it with a group of bikers who liked riding at high speeds late at night.

Though his mother, his marketing agent, and others warned him not to ride the motorcycle, Williams did so anyway. On June 19, 2003, after playing just one season with the Bulls, Williams crashed his motorcycle into a pole and nearly died.

Coach K was one of the first to visit him in the hospital and took Williams' hand.

Despite grogginess from painkillers, Williams immediately knew it was Krzyzewski. Williams describes the moment, "I was overwhelmed with emotion — my second father had arrived."[104]

Williams then began to cry, telling Coach K he would never play again. Krzyzewski reached into his pocket, took out his mother's rosary-bead pendant and gave it to Williams. "Give this back to me when you play again, because you are going to play again," he said.

Krzyzewski and Duke helped Williams transfer to a hospital near the university in Durham, North Carolina. Williams rented a house near the Krzyzewskis. Former Duke teammates texted, came to hang out, and pushed his wheelchair around, continuing as the family they became as teammates.

Coach K stopped by occasionally and assessed his jump shot once he could shoot again.

Williams summed up why Krzyzewski was so valuable to him. "He always gives every ounce of himself to you to help you become the best version of yourself. It doesn't stop when you are done playing for him. If you need him, he's there without you having to ask. That's a man. That's a coach."[105]

That's the leadership, level of dedication, and coaching you want for your brand to help it move past adolescence.

## Independence Changes Everything, Including Curfews

Anyone who guides an adolescent has to realize when to give them independence. For my parents, it was the minute I went to college.

Thanksgiving of my freshman year was the first time I returned home. My high school friend group was gathering two towns away. I asked to have the car for the evening. My father handed me the keys and asked when I thought I would be home.

I was in no mood to be constrained and replied "3 am."

My father said "Okay."

I nearly fell over. And I couldn't leave it alone.

"Wait, what? You're okay with that? After insisting I be home by 12:30 am a few months ago?"

My father replied, "You're not living full-time under our roof anymore. You have your own life. You need to make your own decisions. We've done what we could do to help you make the right ones."

# Key Takeaways from Asserting Independence

- Brands that are asserting their independence are highlighting a leadership problem that is preventing their growth.

- The leadership issue could be that the business leader lacks the skills to help the business grow further, is burned out or is not interested in the management activities that come with a brand that is trying to scale up its growth.

- Leaders who lack the skills but have the interest in continuing to lead the brand can work to acquire the skills through education, coaching, and CEO peer support groups.

- Leaders who realize they are not interested in continuing need to find new leadership for the brand and decide if they will stay in a secondary role or leave entirely.

- As the business leader, if your brand is asserting independence, your honesty with yourself over your true leadership fitness and interest is crucial for the brand to get back to growth and thrive.

# How I Untangled My Brand's Adolescence

n January 2011, I had the epiphany that my brand was having an identity crisis. This was just the beginning.

The more I studied brands in adolescence and brands who were performing well, the more I saw deficiencies in my own brand. Remember how I said that you could remedy one symptom and then discover another? That was me.

With 20/20 hindsight I know my brand not only had an identity crisis, but also had periods where it was self-centered, suffering from FOMO, and oversleeping.

I wish I could tell you navigating my brand's adolescence went smoothly, that I identified each symptom quickly and remedied it on the first try.

But I can't. Not even close.

Much like parenting my children, who hit adolescence at the same time as my brand, I found the process a sequence of surprise discoveries, hoping to make the right decision in the moment, crafting guidelines to improve future situations, and revising those guidelines through subsequent testing and experience. There were mistakes, false starts, frustrations, scrapped attempts, and a fair amount of dark chocolate involved.

Here's how it went down.

## Surprises, Listening, and Iterations

In November 2010, before I had my epiphany and knew how all of this fit together, I did research to understand my brand's attributes. I used the process and exact email I recommended in Chapter 3 to solicit input from clients, colleagues, friends, and family. I also used a 360° personal assessment tool.

Wow, was I surprised at what I got. With my background in consumer insights, I expected my audience to say the first three words that came to mind for me would be "research, organization, professional," or something along those lines. Instead, my top four attributes were "intelligent, thorough, reliable, and trustworthy."

Though they were not what I expected, I was honored. These attributes have served my brand well. In addition to guiding my brand personality, voice, and tone, they have also helped me understand my strengths relative to my competition.

The second component of my brand identity — my purpose — lagged behind.

I started putting together what I called "business plans" in 2010 and 2011. But they weren't business plans. They were to-do lists of marketing tactics I intended to employ during the year. Things like developing a website for my business and building a centralized contact database.

Yes, a marketing consultant without a website until 2010. Did I mention that my brand overslept?

It took until February 2012 for a purpose to show up atop my business plan, and for the plan to include target audiences, objectives, and strategies. But that first purpose was useless: "To establish my thought leadership on the Brands in Adolescence concept, to raise awareness of my business, and to create saleable products/services."

Not only is this meaningless, it is self-centered. It is all about what I wanted and has no insight into how my brand would serve its audience and contribute to the world.

I told you my process was ugly. The only good thing I can say is that this particular purpose did not last long.

By October 2012, I had changed it to: "To help clients grow their business by helping them understand their brand, evolve it in a meaningful way, and profit from it via well-executed marketing strategies and tactics."

Still not specific enough, but at least this was client-centric. It reflects conversations I was having with clients, prospects, connections, and my newsletter readers.

One of the best things I did for my brand in 2012 was launch my Varsity Marketing newsletter. There is nothing like writing to force you to do research and codify your ideas. And the best part? You receive feedback on those ideas. Well, okay, getting new clients and referrals might be tied for best part too.

But back to the feedback from my newsletter. My brand studies and marketing insights prompted conversations with readers that showed me how much they, business owners in particular, anguished over their marketing decisions. Marketing was on the sidelines most of the time, repeatedly falling down their to-do lists whenever anything else popped up.

The perpetual to-do-list sink came less from time constraints and more from their dread of marketing. The more I listened, the more I realized that business owners who had no marketing staff or just one junior person were grasping for marketing strategies and tactics they could invest in, knowing they had a good chance of a meaningful return. Most felt that marketing was like throwing darts blindfolded. The chances of benefiting from the time and money invested were unknown and if you were not careful you could do more harm than good.

I've always loved marketing. It broke my heart that so many business owners who could benefit from it feared and dreaded it.

In 2017, I revised my purpose to: "I help business owners make confident marketing decisions."

This purpose motivates me to my desk every day. This is a difference I can make in the world to ease my audience's stress and help them and their brands be more successful.

## Shedding My Fear of Missing Out

The other thing my newsletter and other brand-in-adolescence conversations did was to help me hone my target audience.

Back in 2012, when I wrote my first real but still lame business plan, I listed four target audiences, two of which I borrowed from HubSpot: Ollie Owner, Mary Marketer, venture capitalists, and referral sources. The story I told myself about these four targets was that they all had connections to brands in adolescence.

But the truth was, trying to target all four groups was too much for a one-person company and diluted my ability to speak specifically to anyone. I had also taken the shortcut of borrowing HubSpot's two buyer personas, thinking I would avoid reinventing the wheel. But that was not a good idea. Those wheels did not fit my brand.

Brand-in-adolescence conversations with clients, prospects, newsletter readers, and fellow conference attendees helped me muster the courage to drop three of those groups and focus on business owners of consumer products companies 5-25 years old that have plateaued. Typically, they have revenues between $2 million-$50 million and 10-150 employees.

## Choosing My Brand's Friends

I've had the honor of working with many business owners who sought to make specific marketing decisions with confidence. Sometimes their brands matched at least some of the typical criteria above. Sometimes not. But not every business owner who called was a good match for my brand. Prospects needed to align with my brand's values as well.

Though I did not write these down until recently, my brand values — which, as a solo professional, are also personal values — have guided my choice of which prospects were a good fit for my brand, and they continue to do so. These values also pertain to partners and collaborators I have worked with. My brand shines only when I can be true to these five values:

1. **Integrity.** Trust is everything in a relationship. To maintain that trust, I feel a fiduciary duty to act in the best interest of my client and to treat their money as I would my own.

   This has meant that I have advised clients against research and consulting projects they have requested that would yield "nice-to-know" information, but not make a real difference to their decision. Sometimes this has cut thousands of dollars from the fee I would have charged them, but it was the right thing to do. I've also pushed clients to spend more when the insights they would gain would substantially increase their likelihood of a better decision and more brand growth.

2. **Clear, straightforward, and transparent communication.** I work best with clients when we are honest and open with each other about the situation we are addressing and about developments as my consulting engagement progresses. The more information clients share upfront, the faster and better I can help. I keep clients' information confidential, with or without a nondisclosure agreement.

   Clients who are amenable to this kind of communication tend to care about their brands so much that they want the truth — even if the truth is not good news. Sometimes it is good news! When it is not, I'm kind in my communication, but I don't sugarcoat things. My job is to help. Soft-pedaling insights dilutes that help.

   A great side benefit of this value is that clients and I often develop friendships that last well beyond the scope of my engagement.

3. **I'm all in.** I learned a long time ago that I can't do half-assed. I don't know how to do something partway. I'm a depth person. If you have a marketing problem, I'm going to get to the heart of it and help you solve it. I only take projects where I can do my best — best thinking, best writing, best analysis. My clients, colleagues, friends, and family must know this already. I think that's how "thorough" rose to the top of my attribute list.

   Not all prospects are interested in the change that solving the problem might involve. They might consider it time-consuming and costly. They don't want a solution, but a band-aid.

   For some, a band-aid might work. I don't know how to

stop at band-aid, so I decline those projects. I'm not afraid of complexity and change, and I want to make a difference. I also know that if I accepted a band-aid project, I'd do the rest of the work anyway because I am curious. And thorough.

4. **I deliver on my promises.** I meet or beat deadlines. I've worked on tight deadlines, but I won't accept a deadline that is not feasible.

   Delivering on my promise also means I accept work I know I can do well. If a prospect or client requests work that's out of my insights, strategy, and writing zone, I'll refer them or bring in a colleague for the services they need. For PR or social media help, for example.

5. **I don't work with anyone I don't like or don't trust.** Life is too short. If my shyster-meter goes off, I'll refer someone elsewhere or just pass.

## A Niche No One Had Heard Of

Beginning in February 2011, I started telling everyone I specialized in brands in adolescence, brands that stall after their initial success. Not only did this attract clients of that ilk, but I quickly became known as the "brands in adolescence" consultant. By design, my focus of study became my niche.

Though I had test-marketed the concept a little, it still felt risky to declare a niche no one had ever heard of. Yet I felt I had little to lose after floundering for so long. If it did not work out, I'd just try again.

Happily, it has worked out.

My brand's adolescence led me on this wonderful path where I met new people, heard great stories, and helped clients get back to growth by establishing meaningful brand guidelines. It led to my monthly newsletter and to speaking engagements.

The brands-in-adolescence concept has been a work in progress for me, like chipping away at a marble block to reveal the statue within. Developing my own brand alongside my studies of other brands has made it easier to decide where to invest my time and money and how to serve my clients best. It has also helped me empathize with my clients, as I've seen how challenging the process can be.

I wrote this book to spare you at least some of the heartache, frustration, time, and expense that I experienced. It is my hope that this book will streamline your experience as you address your brand's adolescence to get it back to growth mode.

## What's Next for Your Brand?

No other brand is exactly like yours. Your brand is charting a never-before-traveled road and there is no one right answer on how to do that.

There are, however, common elements and guidelines that successful brands share, as we have seen in the stories of brands grappling with their adolescence.

Successful brands have:

- A clear **purpose**
- Distinct **attributes** that constitute a unique personality
- **Values** to live and operate by

- A specific **audience** or set of target markets that are large enough for the brand to grow, and a deep knowledge of those markets
- A defined **niche**
- A **strategic plan** that reflects current understanding of the world in which it operates
- An appropriately passionate and skilled leader at the helm

In this book, I've shown you how adolescent symptoms may indicate that one or more of these key elements is missing from your brand or needs course correction. Hopefully you've identified the symptom or symptoms your brand has and can take the steps to remedy them.

It may feel like a daunting task. Just take it one step at a time. Engage your brand team in the work. You don't have to do this all alone. The results will likely be better if you include them.

Though it may be hard work, you may also discover wonderful things about your brand that make working more joyful. Untapped talent and resources. Competitive advantages. New products or audience opportunities. There's plenty of long-term benefit from the investment of time and energy you can make starting right now.

If I can do it, you can do it!

What happens now?

If you know which symptom is plaguing your brand, you can go back to that chapter and begin the action steps to remedy it.

If you are unsure which symptom is plaguing your brand, you can return to the chapter that resonated most and see if that is why.

If you enjoyed this book and would like to receive more

marketing insights monthly, please sign up for my newsletter at estarrassociates.com/newsletter-sign-up.

If you would like additional resources to use as you work through your brand's adolescence, you can find them at estarrassociates.com/brand-adolescence.

I would love to hear from you about your brand journey. My email is evelyn@estarrassociates.com. Or you can find my contact information on my website at estarrassociates.com. I reply to every email. I look forward to hearing what has worked for you.

Wishing you all the joys of parenting your brand and seeing it grow!

# FURTHER READING

For more insight into long-term brand and marketing success, check out some of the books I read while researching this book.

*Marketing Rebellion*, Mark W. Schaefer

*Fusion: How Integrating Brand and Culture Powers the World's Greatest Companies*, Denise Lee Yohn

*Start with Why*, Simon Sinek

*The Infinite Game*, Simon Sinek

*Keep Swinging*, Jay Myers with Darren Dahl

*Hitting the Curveballs: How Crisis Can Strengthen and Grow Your Business*, Jay Myers

*Life is Good: The Book*, Bert and John Jacobs

*What Great Brands Do: The Seven Brand-Building Principles That Separate the Best from the Rest*, Denise Lee Yohn.

# ACKNOWLEDGEMENTS

I n Dan Pink's acknowledgements to his book *When*, he observes that first-time authors "typically thank a preposterously wide circle of contacts." Welp, this *is* my first rodeo. And why cap one's gratitude?

My heartfelt thanks and infinite appreciation to . . .

Chantel Hamilton, my editor, for helping me shape the content of this book and for delivering her help with the perfect mix of enthusiasm, guidance, and instruction. The manuscript traveled lightyears from my initial off-base outline under your watchful eye.

Kirstyn Smith, for her meticulous copyediting.

Chris Bond, for reading and providing unfiltered feedback on my manuscript, despite trying personal circumstances. You rock!

All the business owners who shared their stories and answered my questions with candor and generosity. Special thanks to: Mary Adams, Jenna Avery, Stephanie Blackwell, Spenser Brosseau, Erin Calvo-Bacci, Stacy DeBroff, Lucy Dearborn, Naomi Dunford, Arielle Freedman, Barbara Freedman, Ron Freedman, Veronica Guarino (Geeg too), Leslie Kerr, Lisa Magaro, Bob Monahan, Jay Myers, Howie Sonnenschein, and Bob Van Andel. Your journeys inspired me. Your patience helped me get it right.

My newsletter readers, for their questions, comments, and ideas that have furthered my thinking and fueled my energy to keep publishing.

My Called-to-Write friends, who welcomed me to their community and cheered me on writing sprint after writing sprint, especially Jenna Avery, Leesa Brown, Emilie Portell, Rebecca Brams, Sarah Newman, and Mary Montanye. Jenna, your coaching helped me build my writing muscle and complete the first draft. Mary, your wise advice "The Muse doesn't care about right" enabled me to belt out my words without fear.

Cathy Elcik, who introduced me to many new writer friends and welcomed me to the table literally at the Muse and the Marketplace and AWP and figuratively in online groups. Your friendship, humor, insights, and support have been a lifeline to my writing and a great source of joy. I'll research to procrastinate for you anytime.

The Wonder NaNo group, especially Crystal King, Anjali Mitter Duva, Katrin Schumann, and Jeannie McWilliams Blasberg for writing sprint company, camaraderie, and answering my novice questions.

Ann Handley, for helping me choose my title. Your compassion and support minimized my angst. Your warmth and brave writing inspire me.

Mark Schaefer, for his generous book marketing advice and friendship.

Jill Ebstein, for sharing her writing and self-publishing experience. Your frequent encouragement makes me feel amazing.

Andrea Novakowski, for years of peer support and friendship.

My OG book club members, Kristen Herbert, Chitra Satyaprasad Mills, Regina Wu, Diana Hwang, and Wendy Wayne Mishara, for cheering me on. Badass Moms rule!

And to my family.

Mom and Dad, thank you for your unconditional love and for articulating your belief that I could accomplish anything I set out to do.

Cindy and Ken, my siblings, for your love.

AJ and Fiona, my favorite adolescents in the world now entering adulthood, for your support, love, insights, and help with a few of the cultural aspects of this book. You delight me and make me proud every day.

And to Dan, who read my manuscript and provided crucial feedback, and has been my partner in life for over 26 years. Your insights made this a better book and your partnership has made me a better person. You are, and always will be, the love of my life.

# ABOUT THE AUTHOR

Evelyn J. Starr is a brand expert and writer with over 25 years of marketing strategy and research experience. Evelyn uses her keen powers of observation and insight to help her clients wow their customers and grow their businesses. She specializes in working with Brands in Adolescence, brands that have stalled after their initial success.

Her clients have ranged from small businesses like Laird Superfood and Harbor Sweets to global brands like Hasbro and Gillette.

Before founding E. Starr Associates in 1999, Evelyn worked for some of New England's most recognized brands including Dunkin', Veryfine Products, and The First Years. As leader of

the Care & Safety category at The First Years, she launched one of the company's most successful products, the Hands-Free Gate, which won The National Parenting Seal of Approval in 2002.

Evelyn earned an MBA in Marketing from Boston College's Carroll School of Management and graduated with honors from Vassar College with a BA in Economics and French. Living in the Greater

Boston area, her passions include travel, reading, writing, yoga, tea, dark chocolate and nurturing the entrepreneurial spirit in both her husband and her two children.

You can stay connected and follow along with Evelyn at www .estarrassociates.com, on LinkedIn, and on Twitter: @EvelynJStarr.

# ENDNOTES

## Chapter 1: A Brief Bit about Brands and Brand Adolescence

1. Smith, J. David, Zakzewski, Alexandria C., Johnson, Jennifer M., Valleau, Jeanette C. 2016. "Ecology, Fitness, Evolution: New Perspectives on Categorization." *Current Directions in Psychological Science.* 25, no. 4 (August): 266-274. https://permanent.link/to/teenage-wastebrand/doi-org-10-1177-0963721416652393

2. Court, David, Dave Elzinga, Susan Mulder and Ole Jørgen Vetvik. 2009. "The Customer Decision Journey," McKinsey Quarterly, June 1, 2009. https://permanent.link/to/teenage-wastebrand/www-mckinsey-com-business-functions-marketing-and-sales-our-insights-the-consumer-decision-journey

3. Schaefer, Mark W. 2019. *Marketing Rebellion: The Most Human Company Wins*, p. 35.

## Chapter 2: Scenarios That May Masquerade as Brand Adolescence, but Are Not

4. LaPorte, Nicole. 2009. "DVD Sales Way Down; Hi-Def Slow to Rescue." *The Wrap*, February 15, 2009. https://permanent.link/to/teenage-wastebrand/www-thewrap-com-dvd-sales-way-down-high-def-slow-rescue-1404

5. Interview with Mary Adams, June 6, 2018.

6. Interview with Stacy DeBroff, October 4, 2018.

7. Interview with Stacy DeBroff, October 4, 2018.

8. Interview with Stacy DeBroff, October 4, 2018.

## Chapter 3: Having an Identity Crisis

9.  Hughes, John, writer and director. 1985. *The Breakfast Club.* Universal Pictures.

10.  Garrard, Cathy. N.d. "Big Idea: Meet the Creator of Crocs." *Parents* Magazine. https://permanent.link/to/teenage -wastebrand/www-parents-com-kids-style-fashion-crocs

11.  Business Wire. 2007. "Crocs Inc. Reports Fiscal 2006 Fourth Quarter and Year End Results," February 20, 2007. https:// www.businesswire.com/news/home/20070220006361/en/ Crocs-Reports-Fiscal-2006-Fourth-Quarter-Year-End

12.  Piedra, Xavier. 2018. "The Croc-pocalypse may be upon us and people have mixed feelings about it." *Mashable*, August 9, 2018. https://permanent.link/to/teenage-wastebrand/ mashable-com-article-crocs-closing-twitter-reactions

13.  Ogden, Cody. 2021. "Killed by Google." Accessed February 9, 2021. https://permanent.link/to/teenage-wastebrand/ killedbygoogle-com

14.  Interview with Naomi Dunford, July 17, 2018.

15.  Interview with Mary Adams, June 6, 2018.

16.  Kenny, Graham. 2014. "Your Company's Purpose Is Not Its Mission, Vision or Values." *Harvard Business Review*, September 3, 2014. https://permanent.link/to/teenage-wastebrand/hbr-org- 2014-09-your-companys-purpose-is-not-its-vision-mission-or-values

17.  Sinek, Simon. "Why Discovery Course." *Find Your Why*, course taken November 2016.

18.  Sweetgreen. 2020. Our Story page, accessed July 29, 2020. https://permanent.link/to/teenage-wastebrand/ www-sweetgreen-com-our-story

19.  Jacobs, Bert and John. 2015. *Life Is Good: The Book.* Washington, DC: National Geographic, p. 27.

20.  US Bureau of Labor Statistics. 2020. "Entrepreneurship and the US Economy." Accessed July 29, 2020. https://permanent.link/to/teenage-wastebrand/ bls-gov-bdm-entrepreneurship-entrepreneurship-htm

21.  Interview with Naomi Dunford, July 17, 2018.

22.  Interview with Naomi Dunford, July 17, 2018.

23.  Crocs. 2021. Crocs Investor Presentation, January 11, 2021. https://permanent.link/to/teenage-wastebrand/investors-crocs-com-press-releases-press-release-details-2021-crocs-inc-guides-accelerated-2021-revenue-growth-of-20-to-25-default-aspx

## Chapter 4: Running with the Wrong Crowd

24.  Alcatraz East Crime Museum. 2021. "Tim Allen Mugshot." Accessed February 17, 2021. https://permanent.link/to/teenage-wastebrand/www-alcatrazeast-com-crime-library-celebrity-mugshots-tim-allen-mugshot

25.  Interview with Spenser Brosseau, October 11, 2018.

26.  Gallagher, Billy. 2013. "Founders John Zimmer and Logan Green Explain How Lyft Was Born Out Of Zimride." *TechCrunch*, September 9, 2013. https://permanent.link/to/teenage-wastebrand/ techcrunch-com-2013-09-09-zimmer-green-from-zimride-to-lyft

27.  Godin, Seth. 2018. *This Is Marketing*. New York: Portfolio/ Penguin, p. 28.

28.  The Wedding Report. N.d. "2019 Wedding Statistics for Massachusetts." Accessed July 23, 2020. https://permanent. link/to/teenage-wastebrand/wedding-report-index-cfm-action-wedding_statistics-view-market-id-25-idtype-s-location-massachusetts

29.  Statista. N.d. "Marriage rate in Massachusetts from 1990-2018." Accessed July 23, 2020. https://

permanent.link/to/teenage-wastebrand/
www-statista-com-statistics-206965-marriage-rate-in-massachusetts

30.  The Knot. N.d. "Everything You Need to Know About Getting Married in Massachusetts." Accessed July 23, 2020. https://www. theknot.com/content/massachusetts-wedding-planning-tips

## Chapter 5: Acting Self-Centered

31.  Frenkel, Sheera and Kevin Roose. 2018. "Zuckerberg, Facing Facebook's Worst Crisis Yet, Pledges Better Privacy." *New York Times*, March 21, 2018. https://permanent.link/to/teenage-wastebrand/www-nytimes-com-2018-03-21-technology-facebook-zuckerberg-data-privacy-html

32.  Frenkel, Sheera, Nicholas Confessore, Cecilia Kang, Matthew Rosenberg and Jack Nicas. 2018. "Delay, Deny and Deflect: How Facebook's Leaders Fought Through Crisis." *New York Times*, November 14, 2018. https://permanent.link/to/teenage-wastebrand/www-nytimes-com-2018-11-14-technology-facebook-data-russia-election-racism-html

33.  Facebook, Inc. FY-14-Q1 Form 10Q for the period ending March 31, 2014 (filed April 25, 2014) p. 46, from SEC website, https://permanent.link/to/teenage-wastebrand/www-sec-gov-archives-edgar-data-1326801-000132680114000023-fb-3312014x10q-htm

34.  Facebook. 2021. "Facebook Reports Fourth Quarter and Full Year 2020 Results." January 27, 2021. https://permanent.link/to/teenage-wastebrand/investor-fb-com-investor-news-press-release-details-2020-facebook-reports-fourth-quarter-and-full-year-2019-results-default-aspx

35.  Facebook. "Facebook Careers." Accessed July 21, 2020. https://permanent.link/to/teenage-wastebrand/m-facebook-com-facebookcareers-photos-tabalbumandalbum_id1655178611435493and_rdr

36.  Newton, Casey. "Zuckerberg: The idea that fake news on Facebook influenced the election is 'crazy'." *The Verge*, November

10, 2016. https://permanent.link/to/teenage-wastebrand/www-theverge-com-2016-11-10-13594558-mark-zuckerberg-election-fake-news-trump

37. Zuckerberg, Mark. "Building Global Community." Facebook, February 16, 2017. https://permanent.link/to/teenage-wastebrand/m-facebook-com-nt-screen-paramspercent7bpercent22note_idpercent22percent3a370797109 5882612percent7dandpathpercent2fnotespercent2fnotepercent2f and_rdr

38. Weissman, Cale Guthrie. "It turns out Facebook actually did want to sell your data." *Fast Company*, November 29, 2018. https://permanent.link/to/teenage-wastebrand/www-fastcompany-com-90273971-it-turns-out-facebook-actually-did-want-to-sell-your-data

39. Zuckerberg, Mark. 2018. "Mark Zuckerberg in his own words: The CNN Interview." Interview by Laurie Segall. *CNN Business*, CNN, March 21, 2018. https://permanent.link/to/teenage-wastebrand/money-cnn-com-2018-03-21-technology-mark-zuckerberg-cnn-interview-transcript-index-html

40. Notopoulos, Katie. 2019. "Burt's Bush and XXXTentacion's Death: Why Facebook Moderators Fail." *BuzzFeed News*, September 23, 2019. https://permanent.link/to/teenage-wastebrand/www-buzzfeednews-com-article-katienotopoulos-facebook-moderators-are-set-up-to-fail

41. McFarland, Matt. 2018. "Segway was supposed to change the world. Two decades later, it just might." *CNN Business*, October 30, 2018. https://permanent.link/to/teenage-wastebrand/www-cnn-com-2018-10-30-tech-segway-history-index-html

42. McFarland, Matt. 2018. "Segway was supposed to change the world. Two decades later, it just might." *CNN Business*, October 30, 2018. https://permanent.link/to/teenage-wastebrand/www-cnn-com-2018-10-30-tech-segway-history-index-html

43. Sinek, Simon. 2019. *The Infinite Game*, United States of America: PenguinRandomHouse LLC., pp 131-142.

44. Perrin, Andrew. 2018. "Americans are changing their relationship with Facebook." *Pew Research Center*, September 5, 2018. https://permanent.link/to/teenage-wastebrand/www-pewresearch-org-fact-tank-2018-09-05-americans-are-changing-their-relationship-with-facebook

45. Holley, Peter. 2018. "Lime blamed its fire-prone batteries on Segway's manufacturing. Now Segway is pushing back." *The Washington Post*, November 2, 2018. https://permanent.link/to/teenage-wastebrand/www-washingtonpost-com-technology-2018-11-02-lime-blamed-their-fire-prone-batteries-segways-manufacturing-now-segway-is-pushing-back

46. Hsieh, Tony. 2010. "Your culture is your brand," *HuffPost*, November 15, 2010, updated December 6, 2017. https://permanent.link/to/teenage-wastebrand/www-huffpost-com-entry-zappos-founder-tony-hsieh_1_b_783333

47. Yohn, Denise Lee. 2018. *Fusion: How Integrating Brand and Culture Powers the World's Greatest Companies.* Boston: Nicholas Brealey Publishing, pp 39-42.

48. Coyne, Kevin P. and Shawn T. Coyne. 2011 "Seven steps to better brainstorming." *McKinsey Quarterly*, March 1, 2011. https://permanent.link/to/teenage-wastebrand/www-mckinsey-com-business-functions-strategy-and-corporate-finance-our-insights-seven-steps-to-better-brainstorming

49. Constine, Josh. 2020 "Facebook asks for a moat of regulations it already meets." *Extra Crunch*, February 17, 2020. https://permanent.link/to/teenage-wastebrand/techcrunch-com-2020-02-17-regulate-facebook

## Chapter 6: Suffering from FOMO and Trying Too Hard to Fit In

50. Przybylski, Andrew K., Kou Murayama, Cody DeHaan, and Valerie Gladwell. 2013. "Motivational, Emotional, and Behavioral Correlates of Fear of Missing Out." *Computers in Human Behavior* 29, no. 4 (July): 1841-1848. https://permanent.link/to/

teenage-wastebrand/www-sciencedirect-com-science-article-abs-pii-s0747563213000800-viapercent3dihub

51. Australian Psychological Society. 2015. "Teens Suffer Highest Rate of FOMO," November 8, 2015, https://permanent.link/to/teenage-wastebrand/psychology-org-au-news-media_releases-8nov2015-fomo

52. Interview with Erin Calvo-Bacci, May 29, 2018.

53. Interview with Erin Calvo-Bacci, May 29, 2018.

54. Brandz. 2020. "Top 100 Most Valuable Global Brands 2020." https://permanent.link/to/teenage-wastebrand/www-brandz-com-admin-uploads-files-2020_brandz_global_top_100_report-pdf

55. Google. 2020. "Ten things we know to be true." About Google. Accessed July 30, 2020. https://permanent.link/to/teenage-wastebrand/www-google-com-about-philosophy-html

56. Ogden, Cody. 2021. "Killed by Google." Accessed February 9, 2021. https://permanent.link/to/teenage-wastebrand/killedbygoogle-com

57. Google Official Blog. 2013. "A second spring of cleaning." March 13, 2013. https://permanent.link/to/teenage-wastebrand/googleblog-blogspot-com-2013-03-a-second-spring-of-cleaning-html

58. Interview with Erin Calvo-Bacci, May 29, 2018.

## Chapter 7: Needing to Make New Friends

59. Denworth, Linda. 2020. "The Outsize Influence of Your Middle School Friends." *The Atlantic*, January 28, 2020. https://permanent.link/to/teenage-wastebrand/www-theatlantic-com-family-archive-2020-01-friendship-crucial-adolescent-brain-605638

60. Young, Karen. N.d. "They'll Do What? The What and the Why of the Changes that Come with Adolescence." *Hey Sigmund*. Accessed July 30, 2020. https://permanent.link/to/teenage-wastebrand/

www-heysigmund-com-what-you-need-to-know-about-the-adolescent-brai

61.  Myers, Jay with Darren Dahl. 2007. *Keep Swinging: An Entrepreneur's Story of Overcoming Adversity and Achieving Small Business Success.* Garden City, NY: Morgan James, p.19.

62.  Interview with Jay Myers, May 16, 2018.

63.  Myers, Jay with Darren Dahl, *Keep Swinging: An Entrepreneur's Story of Overcoming Adversity and Achieving Small Business Success*, p.35.

64.  Interview with Jay Myers, May 16, 2018.

65.  Myers, Jay. 2014. *Hitting the Curveballs: How Crisis Can Strengthen and Grow Your Business.* New York: Morgan James, p. 19-20.

66.  Myers, Jay with Darren Dahl, *Keep Swinging: An Entrepreneur's Story of Overcoming Adversity and Achieving Small Business Success*, p.16.

67.  Interview with Lucy Dearborn, September 24, 2018.

68.  Interview with Lucy Dearborn, September 24, 2018.

69.  Myers, Jay, *Hitting the Curveballs: How Crisis Can Strengthen and Grow Your Business*, p. 87.

## Chapter 8: Defending Your Varsity Team Spot

70.  JockBio. N.d. Carmelo Anthony Biography. Accessed July 30, 2020. https://permanent.link/to/teenage-wastebrand/jockbio-com-bios-anthony-anthony_bio-html

71.  Interview with Stephanie Blackwell, September 11, 2018.

72.  Whatley, Sally. 2016. "Spotify's core values." Spotify HR Blog. https://permanent.link/to/teenage-wastebrand/hrblog-spotify-com-2016-09-02-spotifys-core-values

73.  Singh, Manish. 2019. "Spotify hits 108M paying users and 232M overall, but its average revenue per user declines." *TechCrunch,*

July 31, 2019. https://permanent.link/to/teenage-wastebrand/
techcrunch-com-2019-07-31-spotify-108-million

74.  Spotify. 2021. Company info. Accessed February 11,
2021. https://permanent.link/to/teenage-wastebrand/
newsroom-spotify-com-company-info

75.  Singh, Manish, *TechCrunch*, July 31, 2019.

76.  Neely, Amber. 2020. "Amazon Music gaining on Spotify & Apple
Music, with 55 million subscribers globally." *Apple Insider*, January
22, 2020. https://permanent.link/to/teenage-wastebrand/www-
theverge-com-2019-5-8-18537261-google-youtube-music-play-music-
15-million-subscribers

77.  Welch, Chris. 2019. "Google's music apps have reportedly
passed 15 million subscribers." *The Verge*, May 8, 2019. https://
permanent.link/to/teenage-wastebrand/www-theverge-com-
2019-5-8-18537261-google-youtube-music-play-music-15-million-
subscribers

78.  Boulton, Clint. 2016. "How Fedex is Shaving Millions From Its
IT Costs," *CIO*, November 23, 2016. https://permanent.link/to/
teenage-wastebrand/www-cio-com-article-3144504-how-fedex-is-
shaving-millions-from-its-it-costs-html

79.  Fedex. "Fedex History." Accessed July 30, 2020.
https://permanent.link/to/teenage-wastebrand/
www-fedex-com-en-us-about-history-html

80.  Smart Passive Income. 2018. "Income Reports." Accessed April
26, 2019. https://permanent.link/to/teenage-wastebrand/
www-smartpassiveincome-com-category-income-reports

81.  Beer, Jeff. 2018. "Exclusive: "Patagonia is in business to save
our home planet." *Fast Company*, December 13, 2018. https://
permanent.link/to/teenage-wastebrand/www-fastcompany-com-
90280950-exclusive-patagonia-is-in-business-to-save-our-home-
planet

82.  The Walmart Digital Museum. N.d. "Every Day Low Prices."

Accessed July 31, 2020. https://permanent.link/to/teenage-wastebrand/one-walmart-com-content-walmartmuseum-en_us-timeline-decades-1970-artifact-2480-html

## Chapter 9: Oversleeping

83.  Rosenblatt, Bill. 2018. "Google Sells Zagat to The Infatuation, Freeing It to Become Relevant Again," *Forbes*, March 6, 2018. https://permanent.link/to/teenage-wastebrand/www-forbes-com-sites-billrosenblatt-2018-03-06-google-sells-zagat-to-the-infatuation-freeing-it-to-become-great-again-sh4d59a9e14428

84.  Carr, Austin. 2010. "Blockbuster Bankruptcy: A Decade of Decline." *Fast Company*, September 22, 2010. https://permanent.link/to/teenage-wastebrand/www-fastcompany-com-1690654-blockbuster-bankruptcy-decade-decline

85.  "In a few years, Blockbuster goes from dominant to besieged." *Mercury News*, June 18, 2010. https://permanent.link/to/teenage-wastebrand/www-mercurynews-com-2010-06-18-in-a-few-years-blockbuster-goes-from-dominant-to-besieged

86.  Sandoval, Greg. 2011. "Former Blockbuster CEO Tells His Side of Netflix Story." *CNET*, May 25, 2011. https://permanent.link/to/teenage-wastebrand/www-cnet-com-news-former-blockbuster-ceo-tells-his-side-of-netflix-story

87.  Reeves, John. 2012. "9 Fascinating Things About Reed Hastings and Netflix." *The Motley Fool*, November 12, 2012. https://permanent.link/to/teenage-wastebrand/www-fool-com-investing-general-2012-11-12-9-fascinating-things-about-reed-hastings-and-netfl-aspx

88.  Abril, Danielle. 2018. "Former CEO Jim Keyes: Why Blockbuster Really Died and What We Can Learn From It." *D Magazine*, April 6, 2018. https://permanent.link/to/teenage-wastebrand/www-dmagazine-com-business-economy-2018-04-former-ceo-jim-keyes-why-blockbuster-really-died-and-what-we-can-learn-from-it

89.  Baskin, Jonathan Salem. 2013. "The Internet Didn't Kill

Blockbuster, The Company Did It To Itself." *Forbes*, November 8, 2013. https://permanent.link/to/teenage-wastebrand/www-forbes-com-sites-jonathansalembaskin-2013-11-08-the-internet-didnt-kill-blockbuster-the-company-did-it-to-itself-sh1fb251b46488

## Chapter 10: Asserting Independence

90. Beard, Alison. 2017. "Life's Work: An Interview with Mike Krzyzewski." *Harvard Business Review*, March-April 2017, p. 164. https://permanent.link/to/teenage-wastebrand/hbr-org-2017-03-mike-krzyzewski

91. Williams, Jay. 2016. "Jay Williams details his relationship with Coach K." *ESPN*, January 22, 2016. https://permanent.link/to/teenage-wastebrand/www-espn-com-mens-college-basketball-story-_-id-14619998-ncb-jay-williams-life-not-accident-memoir-reinvention

92. Bernstein, Viv. 2015. "Shade of Coach K: Players, Coaches, Media Reflect as Legend's 1000th Win Nears." Bleacher Report, January 23, 2015. https://permanent.link/to/teenage-wastebrand/bleacherreport-com-articles-2339304-shades-of-coach-k-players-coaches-media-reflect-as-legends-1000th-win-nears

93. Rifkin, Glenn. 2007. "Millions in Sales from 3 Simple Words." *The New York Times*, November 22, 2007. https://permanent.link/to/teenage-wastebrand/www-nytimes-com-2007-11-22-business-smallbusiness-22sbiz-html

94. Eng, Dinah. 2014. "Life is good in the T-shirt business." Fortune, May 1, 2014. https://permanent.link/to/teenage-wastebrand/fortune-com-2014-05-01-life-is-good-in-the-t-shirt-business

95. Jacobs, Bert. 2015. "Lessons from Life is Good brand." Interview by Tyler Mathisen and Marcus Lemonis. *CNBC*, November 11, 2015. Video, 4:50. https://permanent.link/to/teenage-wastebrand/www-cnbc-com-video-2015-11-11-lessons-from-life-is-good-brand-html

96. Hoffman Reid. 2013. "If, Why and How Founders Should Hire a 'Professional CEO." *LinkedIn*, January 23, 2013. https://

permanent.link/to/teenage-wastebrand/www-linkedin-com-pulse-20130123161202-1213-if-why-and-how-founders-should-hire-a-professional-ceo

97.  Hoffman Reid. 2013. "If, Why and How Founders Should Hire a 'Professional CEO." *LinkedIn*, January 23, 2013. https://permanent.link/to/teenage-wastebrand/www-linkedin-com-pulse-20130123161202-1213-if-why-and-how-founders-should-hire-a-professional-ceo

98.  Clay Collins. 2017. "John Tedesco Will Succeed Me as CEO (But I'm Taking on a New Role at Leadpages)." *LeadPages*, July 27, 2017. https://permanent.link/to/teenage-wastebrand/www-leadpages-com-blog-john-tedesco-ceo-leadpages

99.  Jacobs, Bert. 2015. "Lessons from Life is Good brand." Interview by Tyler Mathisen and Marcus Lemonis. *CNBC*, November 11, 2015. Video, 4:50. https://permanent.link/to/teenage-wastebrand/www-cnbc-com-video-2015-11-11-lessons-from-life-is-good-brand-html

100.  Rifkin, Glenn. 2007. "Millions in Sales from 3 Simple Words." *The New York Times*, November 22, 2007. https://permanent.link/to/teenage-wastebrand/www-nytimes-com-2007-11-22-business-smallbusiness-22sbiz-html

101.  Hoffman Reid. 2013. "If, Why and How Founders Should Hire a 'Professional CEO." *LinkedIn*, January 23, 2013. https://permanent.link/to/teenage-wastebrand/www-linkedin-com-pulse-20130123161202-1213-if-why-and-how-founders-should-hire-a-professional-ceo

102.  Williams, Jay. 2016. *Life is Not an Accident: A Memoir of Reinvention.* New York: HarperCollins, p. 6.

103.  Williams, Jay. 2016. "Jay Williams recalls the fateful day when he 'threw it all away'." *ESPN*, January 21, 2016. https://permanent.link/to/teenage-wastebrand/www-espn-com-mens-college-basketball-story-_-id-14619998-ncb-jay-williams-life-not-accident-memoir-reinvention

104.  Williams, Jay. 2016. *Life is Not an Accident: A Memoir of Reinvention*, p. 25.

105.  Williams, Jay. 2016. *Life is Not an Accident: A Memoir of Reinvention*, p. 25-26.

# INDEX

CPSIA information can be obtained
at www.ICGtesting.com
Printed in the USA
LVHW091437270421
685707LV00019B/305/J